to the child i was who never thought he
would find his way. we did. we made it.

-karnes-

MUJO

-A Book of Everything-

LIFE

I have not always been the best at letting go of things or moving on when I knew I should. The permanence of life has been trimmed off since I have aged to this point in my life. We are all in constant motion, and with that, nothing remains as it is for too long. If it were any different, we would never learn anything. We would never feel anything. We would never understand the value of loss of any kind on any type of scale. To live life to the fullest, is to embrace change. It is a simplistic approach to impermanence. It is easier said than done. I am sure of it. If we do not, we will suffer down the road, as well as share and take part in our suffering with anyone around us. To be human, means to be born already in the process of dying. It means to have your heart fucking broken into a million unrecognizable pieces all at once. It means to give your life in the name of adventure and purpose. Living is difficult on its own. We do not need to add onto it by committing acts of small violence and sabotage on a larger scale for the sake of saving face for things that will not matter or hold space for us later on. I am the worst when it comes to any form of self-sabotage. It has been a friend and lover of mine since I was a kid. We have been through so much together, and none of it turned out the way I had hoped it would. It has cost me almost everything good and true in my life. No one can escape it once it becomes who you are. It is the self-defense mechanism we cling to, because it is familiar for us to feel chaos after years and years of being around nothing but the madness. Becoming who we are will never happen over-night. It will always take us becoming a thousand different versions of ourselves in the process. I have never fit into the narrative of life itself. I have a tendency of writing myself out of my own as it is. Each and every relationship I have ever found myself in, ultimately ended prematurely based on my own consumption for immense wreckage and collateral damage. I was raised on it. I was raised by it on a daily basis. If you continually see something over and over again, the pattern becomes the repetition. From there, your entire foundation is laid and layered over time. It took my over twenty-five years to realize that life is nothing but change. That life is the nothing without finding something to change for, because if we remain the same forever, we will never experience it for what it is and why we were born in the first place. To embrace it, means opening yourself up to alternative endings you never thought could have been possible. The differences between you and I are the reasons why we must continue searching for the possibility of understanding all of it on a macro-level, instead of the micro-living we have been accustomed to. If you wish to live in your circle of comfort, by all means, have at it, but you will not see me asking to join you in any shape or form. There is too much out in the world that is unknown. We know more about the moon than we do the ocean. We know more about mental illness than we do the medicinal side of it. We have statistics for everything these days that try and tell us how to live our lives. The graph hardly ever changes for those who follow the guidelines of it. I never dreamt about a home with a fence around it. I never dreamt of a family of my own. All I wanted was for my family to become one. Slowly over the years, we have found ways to be closer and more loving. It was a tiresome act living as though everything was okay when deep down, nothing inside of my body felt as if it was in the correct place. I write my books and spew out whatever it is that finds me on any given day. I cannot go a single day without writing something down to get it out of me. If I do not, it will fester inside of me, causing me to feel worthless when I know that is the furthest thing from the truth. In this journey, nothing is ever complete. Nothing is ever as bad as it feels to you in the exact moment you are living it. I remember getting my truck impounded back in 2009. My father had to fly from Texas to North Carolina to get it, then drove it all the way back to Texas. It was my second DUI in three months, which I have spoken about before in my books. I am not ashamed of my past because it molded and shaped me into who I am today. I recall that moment specific, because it literally felt I was at my very own rock bottom. But I had not even rolled half-way down the mountain yet. When you realize how much life there is left in this world to live and find, you will begin to cut yourself a little bit of slack after the fact. It is all about perspective, which mine has changed every year I have been alive. This year alone, I thought I would never find a way to get my life back and help my father out of the situation he found himself in. I am still working on it, but it does not take up all of my mind as it once did. Would I like for it to have worked out differently since being back in Texas, yes, but life does not and will never happen on your timeline. It happens when it is meant to be and supposed to happen. Never a second sooner. Most of my life has been formed by the perception of what could be, instead of how things were at the moment. To never lose hope in this fanatical world may be the greatest superpower one can acquire or be born with. Maybe it was my stubbornness that allowed it to take over my life, or maybe I was simply tired of life fucking me over any chance it got. I knew if I could hold my ground a little while longer, one more day at least, things would even themselves out. I felt I held the power to control my environment more than I actually had control over my own actions.

Valuing your own life makes the ultimate difference in anything you do. For me, it took a few decades to arrive to that conclusion, but I did when it mattered the most. I lost religion in 2008. I found my spiritualism shortly after, but my soul already knew of its presence since I was five or six. Life felt different for me as a kid. I saw things, said things, and thought things that were so far out of left field, I kept most of it to myself. A large reason I did, was because I could write about it better than I could verbalize anything. Probably the last thirty years of my life that has been the case. I am getting better at being more vocal towards my needs and desires and just ideas in general. Writing was something more than therapy to me. It was an escapism, an ineffable promise I could keep to my own life to never give up the pursuit of whatever it was that made me happy. Sadly, destruction also makes me content in a lot of ways. I never believed it to be hurtful once it happened. If my truth upset someone, then I knew I was not meant to be in their lives, just as they were not meant to be a part of mine. The last relationship I was in, she had two kids. One of which was living with her. He was around nine at the time. I had never been with someone who had kids, so I thought the only way to know if you could make it work was to be around them. I do not see how you could make it work any other way if you do not meet the kid(s) first and spend quality time around them. At the end of my stay, I felt as though I could not take on the responsibility of a child. I loved the woman I was with dearly, but you cannot stay in a relationship when you know it is not where you need to put yourself for good. It broke her heart, as it did mine to have to tell her that. I wanted it to work. I wanted us to be a family. Especially after she had opened her entire fucking world to me as she did. I felt like the biggest piece of shit, because I could not offer anything more than I already had. I thought I was ready for it all, but I knew if I went through with it, it would eventually end up becoming the biggest regret of my life. Months passed afterwards, and my heart was beginning to change its course. I had thought about nothing but her and her kids the last several months upon leaving her that evening. As I mentioned previously, life does not happen when you want it to, and it showed me again why it will remain that way. I want to say six months had gone by, and we began talking again. Then, tragedy found her and I had no idea to what degree it did. I found out through another friend what had actually happened. The woman I was talking to, she had been talking to a guy on and off for a while before I was in the picture. I am not entirely sure how factual things were after I left her, but I believe they saw each other a few times. One of those times was before her and I were actually together, the guy ended up messaging me on Instagram, telling me all kinds of crazy things, at least to me they were absurd. I told her about it. She said to just block him. Which I did. Valentine's Day that particular year, I was in the kitchen with her and we were getting things ready for dinner. He showed up at the door with flowers and candy. She goes outside to meet him before he walked inside. That was the same week I told her I could not stay and be with her to try and make it work with her and the children. Once you know something is off, you better go through with it and leave the situation or stop it from happening altogether. The intuition, the gut instinct, the feeling of nothing but absolute know with all. If you do not listen to those, you will go down roads and paths you never should have found or ventured down to begin with. I learned to trust those more over the last decade plus of my life. Thankfully, I did not try and refute them in a way I would have before that time period in my life. When I thought her and I were back on solid ground and terms, life happened. It cut in again to show me the situation was not for me and lies had been told up until that point after I was lambasted by her for lying to her, which was never the case. Months went by again before I heard from her. The next time we spoke, she called me and told me she was getting married. I was actually going to ask her to marry me before tragedy found her and she ghosted me. I was happy for her and congratulated her for finding someone who wanted to be in her life forever. She ended up being highly irritated and upset at me for not showing more emotion and trying to win her back. Once someone asks you to marry them, and you say yes, you have already made the choice for us that we were not going to be enough or good enough for you. Such is life when all you want is to find love and have love in your own life when the time is right for you to do so. I have thought about that moment a few times this past year. I have thought how fortunate for it to have worked out as it did. Even though I will remain sending her love and best wishes since what happened to her took place. No one deserves to have their heart crushed and broken as hers did. We all must heal ourselves before we take on any form of everlasting love. If we are not ready and whole, still tending to our wounds and scars, we will become the darkness they were trying to run from all this time. In the same breath, if you find yourself in love with someone who is still trying to do that in their own life, you will take up all of their darkness and they will devour every ounce of light you thought you once had. We cannot continue sacrificing for those who are and will never be ready to do the same for us. It is an alarming game to play, and not something you want to see if you can do just to prove to yourself you can. It has happened to me a few in times during this lifetime. It is something I truly and deeply wish I could go back to the beginning of and change. The infinite suffering that always takes place afterwards is not worth it. The lessons it taught me were what I needed, but I could have done without the misery it caused me for years after it all took place. In this journey, all that is asked of us, is for us to be good enough for ourselves. It is all we can ask and hope for in the end before finding someone else to try and tell us what they believe our worth to be. Once you discover it on your own, it makes everything less deadening. You will come out of it more alive than you have ever been before. You will know for good, without uncertainty, that you were born for the right love to find you. You will know how it feels to let your guard down and not live behind walls made of bones and anger for the rest of your time here on this earth. I know I have endless nights when my last though is nothing but regret. The right kind of love mends us all. Love is the one thing keeping most of us from being in a place of absorbed darkened thoughts being restrained by a hopelessness not many can understand. Today is the Marine Corps birthday. 248 years of fighting, honoring, and reminiscing. I have been looking through old photos and writings that go back to the early 2000's. The photos are of my Marine brothers. When I thought about doing this book, I was not sure how I would write it. I typically have a good idea as to how I want to section things off and turn the book into something more than just another poetry book you pick up and skim through. I wanted it to be something more than anything I had done. Even with, SONDER, I tried to do that. I tried to figure out a beautiful balance for things. The more I have thought about it, the more I wanted this book to have three defined parts without the chapters separating it. I will continue with this book beyond Thanksgiving, give or take. I want to see how far I can take this writing scheme and make use of all the memories and writings I have saved and never used before in a lot of ways. Matthew Perry passed away on October 28th. It came to a shock as everyone who found out in the late evening about his death. Social media posts began popping up all over the place about his passing, along with condolences to his family and close friends. Matthew was only fifty-four, but had lived such an abrasive life the last twenty years or so. It had made him age severely. He appeared to be closer to seventy. He died alone in his jacuzzi at his home. Authorities and first responders ended up calling it an accidental drowning. Friends, was and remains a top three show for me all time. Matthew's character in the show, Chandler Bing, is arguably the best character ever in a sitcom. The show is still my comfort show and one I have watched from beginning to end at least six times. Every year at Thanksgiving and the days leading up to it, my brother and I watch all the episodes we can. It has been our tradition for several years now. It is easily one of my favorite parts of the holiday season. Being able to sit around a television and watch the shows and movies that made you laugh and feel every emotion, will always make you feel as if things are okay. They bring you back to when times may have not been the best for you, but they made it the best for you because of their innate ability to make you laugh or cry or feel whatever you needed to feel. The show never fails to allow me to let my guard down and watch in full contentment without worry of what is going on in my personal life. I know the show will live on long after everyone that watched it on television in the 90's and 2000's have passed from this earth. Thanksgiving is coming up next week. I cannot wait to get to my grandmother's house to watch the episodes I already know they will be showing. He will be missed, but at least the show remains there for anyone who will always go out of their way to watch it. Anytime one of your childhood and young adult favorite actor, artist, or any celebrity you grew up watching and you grew up with in that sens, passes suddenly or late in age, it feels as if you have lost someone close, a friend, a relative in a lot of ways. They will never know you or who you were. They will have a spot in your life because of what they helped you through and with in your own life. They made growing up easier.

They gave you the outlet you needed, the laugh and cry as I mentioned previously. You felt understood because you saw, watched, read, and heard someone who felt like you. Someone who spoke like you. Someone who acted as you did. Someone with the same or similar issues and problems. The magic in life, is finding those who you can relate to and may never be able to say, thank you, to them. The pain is real. The grief you feel after they are gone is real. In this world, we are impacted more so by those whom we will never meet, than by those in our current lives. I know I have. Ever since I began watching television and listening to music, along with reading books, each one has cultivated my imagination in a more profound way than by me knowing anyone else. I will end this thought by saying, being fifty-four, a multimillionaire, and being in a jacuzzi when you pass, is not how I hope to die. Death has no favorites. You will never escape the exactness it has in store for you. I only hope Matthew is at peace, and his family is able to find theirs in the coming months and years because the loss of a loved one is a grief that haunts you every single day and night in some type of way. We began a new week today. It is Monday the thirteenth. More rain and clouds. It has been raining since last Thursday and has not let up at all. Maybe a few times here and there and just long enough for me to go into town for groceries and errands. I cannot remember when we had this much rain for the amount of consecutive days. It is depressing to me when it last this long. One reason why I could never live in the PNW. I would love to visit one day, but living there would never be something I would ever aspire to do. The last four days have been enough for me for an entire year's worth of rain to be honest. I do not function well in it. The clouds fog my mind and make it a bit more tedious for me to write. Over the years, I have gotten better at keeping the negative thoughts out of my mind when this sort of weather finds its way to where I am living. It has also been in the low 60's and 50's the last five days, which on top of the rain has made it impossible to get out or do any sort of working out, which is my main source of mental therapy. It provides me that outlet I need to get away from it all for an hour, if not longer. It gives me more inspiration to write and dig deeper for the truth about me and the words behind the soul. This book is coming together beautifully as to how I wanted it to be. Being able to take my time and section it out this way. Being able to look at older writings has been therapeutic in an infinite amount of ways. The progress I see and look back on from when I started writing again to now is astonishing. If we cannot be our own biggest fans, we will never make it to where we want to go. You have to value your progression, your work ethic, your drive, your purpose, all of it. You will never be where you want to in life if you do not know what it took for you to make it there when you do arrive. Life is trivial as it is. I can only hope you find the time to appreciate your own work whenever you can. It does not have to be from an artistic view either. Find happiness in all victories, in the mundane when others find it to be tirelessly wasteful. There is gold to find there. There is a lifetime's worth of treasure to locate within that pile of nothingness others demand you to see as they do. I am happy with my life today. I am happy to see a curved smile I know is real sitting on my face when I stare into the mirror, hoping to see some sort of change for the day. Hope is right here beside me, as I step into the clothes I will be wearing. The black shirt I still wear. The Dickies work pants, I still wear. The Danner boots, I still wear. But the human wearing them is jubilant on the inside even if the clothes reflect someone different. Love for self is in my life for the first time in over five years if I had to really think about it. It has been since I was a kid that I was actually thankful for a day arriving for me to find with wide eyes and hushed grin. There is not a lot going on in my life at this moment. I am still single, still living with my father. I am still working my towards an endgame. I have no idea how it will look like once I get there. I wanted there to be someone with me by now, but life has never been one for appeasement. There needs to be a breakdown or multiple letdowns for any sort of transformation to take place and take root inside of you. I have lost count of my breakdowns at this point. My mind has lost its home numerous times, but I write regardless, because one day it will come back to me without it running away from me as I get closer to it. I feel as though I can always write more, give more, be more than what I have done thus far along my journey. It is a constant mind fuck with me because I expect excellence with my craft. I expect conditioned quality with my human-side. I understand it is impossible to have such high expectations living in the world we all find ourselves in, but it is the perfectionist in me. It is funny, because not everything in my life is regarded that way by me. There is not a higher bar anyone can set for myself than I already have. It has been something I have been trying to reach for over twenty years now. I have failed a million times. I have been the worst person ever a million more. The last several years, I have been working on my forgiveness for all of what I did and still feel like I am paying for. There was never a point in my life when I thought, "Yeah, okay, I will live with my dad for thirty years and take care of him and miss out on any semblance of a life for myself because that makes all the sense to forfeit yours so you can have nothing to show for it at the end of it besides a few books and millions of writings no one may ever read." Grief is something I could spend years writing about. At least for me, it has been one of more poignant areas of my life. I carry more than I should. I have more mountains I have yet to climb, but I continue making a few more just so I have something to reach for once I am over the next one. The view never changes. The mindset never wavers. Each and every day, I am all in with my work and life, which creates a divide in my personal life with anyone I think I could or want to be with. Once you get in-between the ages of thirty and thirty-five, you realize whomever you meet and want to be with will have a child or children by the time you find it all. It will all come down to whether or not you are ready for that kind of addition to your life. I know I was not a few years ago when I had a chance to settle down. I feel as though I may have another opportunity at it in the near future. If we are able to speak things into existence, I hope you take the time to do it for yourself. We deserve happiness, overall happiness. Be it mentally, physically, or personally. Do not go through life wasting breaths on meaningless things and giving away your energy to outcomes that will never happen. By all means, dream and stay dreaming, but do not stay inside of your head every second of it. When it comes to love being in your life, just know one thing, if they want to talk to you, they will make the effort to do so. If they want you in their life, they will show you where and when. The ones who are meant for us in this life, will never make it difficult for you to see it and feel it. Maybe it does not work out for you both in the end, but at least you know you tried and were given the opportunity to sit, lay, and be with someone who showed you why you should never settle for anything less than what you are able to give to someone else tenfold. Since I was a child, I have been fascinated by that aspect of life, along with a variety of other parts. Growing up and being in a broken home for a majority of my life, psychology struck me as something I would want to study when the time came for it. It is why I wanted to go to college in the first place. If it were not for me choosing a college where all of my friends went to, I may have succeeded in that goal of mine, but the party life was something I could never get out of or away from. It pulled me in every single time. The intricacies of the mind will never not be something I am intrigued by. Being a care-taker at an early age, fixates your mind into wanting to know why you are that way and why certain things remain with you all the way to the end of it. The repressed memories. The blackout spots in our minds. The forgetful nature some of us have and are born with. The ability to compartmentalize better than a majority of the population. It is one of the many reasons why I chose to be in the military. My abilities were shown at an early age when I was able to suffer more than most and outlast anyone I was competing against. The entirety of my enlistment did not go as I had hoped, but i was still able to serve my country to the best of my ability without regret of being in a war where I met some of the most courageous humans this world had ever seen or would ever know. I walked out of there not by choice, but by punishment for my own actions, which is something I deal with on a daily basis. I only have a few friends left from my time in the Corps to show for it who stuck by me through it all. I do my best not to live with regret, but when you have lived as many lives as I have, you learn that will be an impossible task to complete. It is part of human nature. It is in our DNA. It is the backbone of being a human being. You will not find a lot of those who will openly talk about it, but the truth is, without our regrets, we would be happy and go lucky, too naive and blind to see why things happen the way they do and why they must happen to us at the exact moment in time. The butterfly effect, which is a scientific phenomenon, is nothing more than the act of the smallest kind, be it getting your coffee, sleeping in later than usual, or something as simple as walking down the street and noticing something different about it in general, being able to change the course of our lives. The nuances of life have the ability to be monumental shifts that will effect the course of history. However simple or complex it is, it has the ability to alter how all life is lived and seen as it once was. I have always been a deep thinker, a conspiracy believer. Someone who rarely sees or takes things at face value. There is always a deeper meaning and purpose behind why things happen the way they do and why humans act the certain way they do around particular situations. I am not sure where it came from within my family tree, but I love that about me even if others do not think much about it. the subtleties of life are what make us our own individual. They are the foundation of who we are. Your choices dictate more than your path. They are your precise endings as well once you come around to acknowledging it. To be content, is to be divinely you. It is the reason for your creation. We go through life hoping to find reasons and avenues to keep us as far away as possible from becoming someone we can love for whatever reason. The path seems to be elongated the more we search for places, things, and people to help us not be ourselves. I know for me, it took a failed suicide, thirty days in rehab, a relapse, and countless other things for me to finally say, "Fuck it. I want my fucking life back, and I want it right fucking now." I became patient with my life instead of being a patient. I became impatient with those in it who were no longer serving me for the betterment of the whole. I chose to lose contact with several friends. I knew those who chose to do the same with me. I was no longer suitable for their journey, but that is life. We lose those we need so we can get to the next phase of our lives. It begins when we are kids. We think we will have the same set of friends and parents for eternity. It takes us a while to realize just how fairy-tale those years of life are for us and how deeply ridiculous it is for anyone to ever believe life will be the constant we hope for it to be at times. The only choices we have in this world, are who stays in our lives and who eventually goes. There is nothing more. There remains nothing less. It has been that simple since the creation of time itself. Death gives us no favors, because it only has and knows of its promises. Love takes no prisoners. It is a choice-based system we did not sign up for, but became a part of with the first breath we took in and let back out into the world to show it, we are here and we are alive. We do not know how long for, but we do know it is up to us to carve out whatever piece of it we can to call our own for however long we do have. I hope you make fewer excuses in the coming year. I hope you finally figure out what it is you want to do with your life and how not to follow someone else because it feels good. You must work on yourself before you can work with someone else. There will be a part of me constantly searching the areas of my life to improve on. Even on days when the rain is coming down, the sky is a darkened mass of nothing, and life does not know how to let go of my throat, I will find something to correct. I must if I want to arrive at a place where I find myself thriving and whole enough to bring in someone else who wishes to be with me at that given time. The learning curve only bends more the older we get. The intensity of its sharpness is abrupt if you are not paying attention to where you are standing when life happens in front of you without your consent, which will be every fucking time. I hope you find yourself ready for life before it finds you unaware of it happening. You must remember and never forget that you are worthy of love, happiness, and a boldness to take on the day set in front of you. You deserve someone who will never question why you are doing what you need to do in order to live a more fully encapsulating life. If you are to ever fail, and you will more than a few times, you will need to recall the times when your face was in the mud and life was suffocating you with all of its might to make you quit. I have a saying I tell myself when I am feeling lower than usual. It goes, "We are never out of the fight." I heard it in a movie, Lone Survivor, when it came out. There are lessons we learn at every corner we take, down every dead end road we may find ourselves on. To be blind to it or hesitant when it appears means you are not ready to go any further than you already are with what it is you call your life. I may be extreme in a lot of ways, but at least I am honest with myself as to why I am this way. I learned the hard way for over thirty years what happens to you if you do not listen to the universe when it calls out to you. I have learned what happens if you piss your fucking life away in your early teenage years and twenties. We do all we can to remain in the "cool" crowd, to remain in touch with those who have done nothing to help us figure out what it is we are missing. I spent too many years filling in void after void with alcohol, drugs, and numbing myself to the point of not caring about living or dying. I have lost too many friends for me not to have changed. I fucking hate that it took losing them to value my life as I do now. I find myself still rushing through it all, but I am more consistent with my approach. There are days when I feel I am not enough. There are days when I do want to throw my own pity party because of how it has not worked out for me. At the end of the day, I have my health, family, and multiple outlets to help me succeed in whatever it is I wish to do. The only easy thing I have ever done was give up on myself once I rolled beneath the mountain I had become due to my inability to help myself the way I have always needed to.

I am here now for me. I know a lot of people cannot say that, which I find to be incredibly sad, especially these times we are living in. If we cannot be there for us, and show up when that is all that is asked from us, no one else will give us the time of day to stand beside who we are and who they see when their eyes go to look for us. Even at an early age, I had a strong intuition and feeling that I was and would always be a giver, a peacemaker, a helper, and a mediator. My grandfather called me, the quiet man. I did not mind being that way, because I knew how to properly reserve my energy and when to use it. I could never help myself though. I spent most, if not all of my time self-destructing. I spent a large majority of my time abusing my body and insides because it is what felt good and helped me cope with everything I was dealing with. It is what could take away the voices in my head and negative thoughts making me spiral out as much as I did. Life was brutal for me for a long time, just as it is for a lot of us who find it damn near impossible to function in a human world when it is the furthest thing we feel like. I never wished for things to be normal, but there was a time when all I wanted was to have a family who loved one another without the fighting and arguing that became my childhood when I was a kid. Maybe that could have helped me and led me down a different path. I know if it would have, I would not be sitting here today typing as I am, creating the books I have done and handed out into the world for others to read. My life's work is a result of my trauma I endured as a kid and later on in life when I found war to be another outlet for me to get my rage out. My destiny had always been the military avenue. I had known that as well at an early age. If it were not for my father stepping in when I was eighteen, I would have gone to Fullujah where who the hell knows what could have happened to me. I have not spoken a lot about my discharge from the Marines Corps, though those who know me well enough, know what happened. Once I got out of rehab after my failed suicide attempt in 2009, I was sober for six months. November of that same year, I relapsed while drinking cheap wine at the house I had been living in with three of my best friends. I do not remember much from that night, but I do recall it being one of the last times I ever spoke to any of those who were there at the house that evening. It all happened so fast in my head. One minute, I was drinking straight from the bottle itself, and the next, I was waking up in the duty hut, being woken up by the guard telling me to get to formation. I remember blacking out at one point after starting a fire somewhere on the property itself. My first sergeant was called out there and showed up. He took me back to base in his yellow hummer. Before all of that took place, I was insulting one of my best friend's girlfriend and giving everyone a hard time. Once I sobered up some time during the next day, I was punished with sixty days barracks restriction, another NJP(Non-Judicial Punishment) along with a few other things. Before any of that had taken place, I had been in court the week before for my second DUI. I ended up having to pay over ten thousand dollars in lawyer/courtroom fees, and serve twenty-four hours of community service, which I did by going to the library on base every day for a few weeks to clean and organize it. I thought I was in the home-stretch of it all. I wore my Charlie uniform to court. The judge had granted me a discharge from my wrongdoings, and I was back on base that same day as happy as I had ever been. I remember it being overcast and raining. That weekend was when I got into trouble and had my third alcohol related incident. The Marines have a three strike policy. If you get into trouble for three of the same violations, they kick you out. No questions asked. You are done with your military career. I had to go to every higher-up and get my ass chewed out by each one of them, telling me how worthless I was and what a sorry excuse for a Marine I had become. The next week, we found out we were going to Afghanistan again in two weeks. It is a weight I still carry to this day knowing how much I let down those in my unit and myself. The feeling of not deploying with your brothers, the ones you trained, bled, and fought with in the deployment prior, is a guilt I hope no one ever has to face. One of the last commanders I had to see told me point blank the main reason I could not go overseas with them was the fact they were afraid when we got back from war the second time, I would be too far gone to help. They did not want to ruin me completely, but they did not know by not allowing me to go with them, I was already dead inside. I vividly remember each one of the faces of my friends the night they left and got onto the buses to go to Cherry Point. To feel worthless is one thing. It is entirely different animal knowing others feel that way about you as well, including your best friends. We all drank heavily while in the Marines. If you did not smoke cigarettes, you ended up doing so. If you did not drink, there was a good chance you would be an alcoholic by the time you got out. It was a frat party every night. Do not get me wrong, not everyone drank and certainly not everyone drank as heavily as most of us did. There were several who could handle their alcohol. I knew I was never one of those though. Moderation was never a friend of mine. By that time in my life, I had been drinking to blackout since I was a teenager. I could never social drink. If we were not drinking and taking shots of whatever was around, there was no point to even drink. Letting those you love, admire, and respect down is something I may never get over completely. There is the "what if" that plays inside of my mind if I had gone over there with my brothers. It was a tough deployment from what I heard and maybe those who kicked me out did me a solid by not allowing me to go with them. But the fact is, my survivor's guilt remains with me and my best friends I knew and fought with are no longer in my life. It is a rude awakening for you to have lived as long as I have and only have one or two good friends to show for it, but such is life. I know how lucky I am to even be alive. Most days, that is enough for me to carry on. Other days, it is the driving force of my motivation. It is what keeps me at full throttle of wanting to be the best at whatever I do, and it definitely keeps my thoughts of becoming one of the greatest writers of this century. Not everything I write will strike a chord with someone. I learned a long time ago, if you end up writing for others and someone else's approval, you will never know who you are as an artist. The quickest death for a creative is doing what everyone else is doing. If you are not consistently creating with honest intentions, you will never succeed at anything you put your mind, body, and soul to. Others may call you a success, but you know deep down how much of a fraudulent act it is to never step outside of your own way to make a path all on your own. Be proud of being a singular force instead of something the masses can cheapen. Be resilient in your pursuit of anything worth setting your soul on fire to feel. You are the reason behind the smile, behind every single emoted belief within you. You are the creation meant for superior things. The kind of which will never leave you, good or bad unfortunately. It is how life works when you begin working for yourself towards the goals you want to achieve. Never beg for someone to love you, to see you, to be any closer than you are to yourself. In order for a lifetime to make sense, we must first make sense of our own pandemonium and misunderstandings of who we are as individuals. I wish there were easier ways to find it all, but it takes love, death, grief, and all of life's siblings to teach us exactly what it all is. Before we hand over our existence to someone else to see if they can help us or lead us further down the road, please, be sure you are ready for a rejection, for a breaking to occur. Nothing here comes easy or cheap. It either costs your time, energy, or life if you are in the pursuit of certain things others never have the balls to go after. I applaud you for your supreme efforts up until now. With all of my sincerity and bravado, I do. One of the hardest things we can do as humans, is get back up after we force ourselves to the ground in an attempt at salvation after the bottom falls out beneath us. You may think digging your grave and hiding in it will keep you away from all of the rest life has in store for you, but it will fucking pull you out by the tongue if it has to so you learn why it happened the way it did. I regret trying to kill myself because of the predicament I put myself in all of those years ago now. I know there was a reason as to why I survived and others who went through it actually did end up dying. Maybe it was a miracle or maybe I did not cut deep enough, but I do know the doctor told me I was only alive by millimeters, and that was after they had already pumped my stomach to get the pills I had taken out of me. This rambling session is nothing more than me providing myself with a journal for others to read and hopefully learn something from. I have never done anything the right way. There was always a reason as to why I did something. The final stage for me seemed to be a short life after experiencing everything I saw and felt during my younger years of living. The 27 club sticks out to me often, because that is how old I thought I would be when my time here ran out. It felt like I was destined for it, and it was the main reason I acted and did what I did. I feared no one or nothing, because neither of those things could be as bad as who I was then. I figured if I spent all nine lives before then, it would amount to some type of fulfillment, a legacy for me to leave behind for others to remember me by. I stopped drinking completely in 2015. I quit smoking cigarettes right after that. I focused all of my energy and every goal towards something more tangible for me to attain. I knew I would never work a real job, some bullshit suit and tie game to fit into a world I never wanted to belong to in the first place. Being who I am now, writing non-stop about anything and everything, gives me more pleasure than a mother's love I was raised to believe I needed, but found it in other places to make up for the hole it ultimately left me with. My sincere gratitude for suffering, is an endless appreciation. Being able to love yourself after every scar, breakdown, arrest, and meltdown you've ever embraced, gives you a certain clarity in this life. I do not recommend going that route though. I am sure there are other fruitful ways to obtain such things without the impact of the totality from all things you had control over. I am not better than you or the next human who thinks like me. I am nothing without my words, my vulnerability, and my unswerving stance on life and life. We are our own kings and queens. We are Picasso, Rilke, Hemingway, Cohen, Rembrandt, Michelangelo, Monet, Jung, and anyone else who lived their entire life hoping to create something new, unusual, wholly individualistic. We are the hunters and gatherers of a generation who have yet to learn how to pick up after themselves. If someone were to ask me what I know, I would tell them without hesitation, love and death are propaganda. No one has control over it. No one can tell you what it feels like unless you have an inkling of an idea of how it feels to be held by someone who has never been able to be held by anyone else their whole life. I have gone many of years rejecting anyone who wanted to be close to me. Not because I did not want them to love me, but because I was afraid of it showing me how to love myself. I was not ready for it. I probably still cannot house it within myself, but I feel the sadness of being alone more now that I am older. Living with a parent who is seventy may change my mindset a bit, seeing him on the recliner as he does, no one to talk to besides me, and living in his own head playing out what ifs all day. Solitude is a majestic beast not everyone can reign in. For me personally, it is when I thrive the most. It is my church, religion, and holy fucking spirit. It is when I can love myself more than ever before, simply because I have the time needed to reflect without feeling anyone else around me. That is not love. That is acceptance. That is reconciling and healing where others had burned you for trying something different. My madness took decades to nurture, and it is something not accepted by everyone. There is a particular way for me to live, create, talk, and act. I do not show it to another unless I feel the connection to them. My memories run together now that I am increasing my age. This one time in sixth grade, I was seated near the back of the classroom, because I did not enjoy reading out loud and up until that point, never had to before in any other grade. The teacher called on me to read, and I was timid as hell, with a mouth that did not want to move. I began reading and before you knew it, I had read the entire chapter almost. It was one of the first times I recall being proud of myself. I remember the smile I had and the light showcasing in my eyes. It all felt tangible and honest. After that moment, I began reading more and more out loud. I began reading anything I could get my hands on. My mother would buy us books as kids, which is where my love for a good book comes from. I do not read just because I want to and or out of boredom. There needs to be a reason and connection to the author or book beforehand. My mother would buy us Robert Lewis Stevenson books such as, 20,000 Leagues Under The Sea and Swiss Family Robinson. The Hardy Boys was another set of books I enjoyed. Goosebumps, Superhero comics, along with certain poetry books always held my attention span. I believe I read my first poetry book when I was six or seven. It was a poem by Leonard Cohen. I think it was the song, Hallelujah. After that, my interest was sparked and alive with a fucking bonfire inside of me needing more of it to feel that way. Reading has not been something I have enjoyed in my later years. I may read one or two books a year, depending on what I find through my poetry searches and what not, but I do not read novels nor any other kind of books. It is funny how some of us are wired to read fifty or a hundred books a year, and others are good to go with less than ten a year. I am the same way when it comes to podcasts. My attention span and way of processing information does not allow me to sit there and listen to someone else talk and speak for that long. I do enjoy watching and finding new YouTube podcasts though. I watch one called, The Shawn Ryan Show. In a lot of ways, I am topic centric, and hyper-focused on certain genres of all media. Be it books, music, or movies. But in the same breath, I am all over the place to them as well. For me to learn anything, I feel as though I have to be hands on, a true visual learner. My memory recall is not what it once was, but I will never forget a face once I see you. I may not be able to tell you your name once you leave and come back a few days later after meeting, but again, it is all about connection. The sun finally came back out today after having almost five consecutive days of rain, clouds, and gloomy weather. It is not good for me to subject myself to those conditions for that long, but sometimes, there is no other alternative for you. You simply have to suffer through it and do the best you can by using your outlets. I am not as creative when the weather gets that way. Before I moved to Utah in 2018, I had gone there for two weeks at the beginning of the year to see for myself how it was and how it may be like to live there. I researched the weather patterns, checked every website I could for the information I needed. Over the next several days, I found out it had over two hundred and fifty days of sunshine, along with all four seasons. It was perfect for me, because I had lived in Texas and North Carolina the last ten years before that. I knew I needed to get away from this place, this state, the ocean, my father, and everything keeping me stagnant. I had been hiding in other people's lives and stories for too long. I knew if I did not get out of it all, I would become someone I would resent for the rest of my life. It may sound harsh to be that way towards yourself, but there comes a time for all of us to check in or check out, and I was not ready to check out to be someone I never wanted to be. Today, I find myself right back at the same point and pain infliction, which may be considered a failure to some, but I remain breathing, and that is a beautiful gift to have. It is something not a lot of humans woke up with today, yesterday, and tomorrow there will be those who will not be able to. I do my best with my perception and perspective on life, just as I know you all do or else you would not have this book in your hands, reading these very words. I hope you find something useful within these pages for your own life. I hope you never stop wandering and searching for things you love deeply and cannot live without. We hold the power we need to change the course of any storm we may find ourselves in. If you allow it to clear and cleanse your path, you will be rewarded for it in the end. Trust me, you will. Even though I am not anywhere close to being where I want to be, there is a monumental shift taking place around me that I can feel. One day, I will have my own place again. I will be able to leave the house and not have to tell anyone where I am going. I will have the freedoms I desperately lack now. We must believe in it first before it finds us. We must continue speaking about it and to ourselves for the right things to find us at the exact time and place they need to. I have not been with anyone in almost three years now. Once you go so long without someone else, you forget what being held feels like, what sleeping in the same bed with someone can feel like, and how precious the night time is once you have someone to share it with. Those morning kisses and embraces are something I miss often. Having someone there next to you as you wake up, is the one thing that can erase a lifetime of loneliness. I enjoy being alone, yes, but if I had a choice to be with someone I loved more than anything else breathing and walking this world, I would choose her every single day I was allowed to say her name. Today is Friday the 17th which is a Friday. There is less than a week left until Thanksgiving. I will be leaving early Tuesday morning to pick up my younger brother at the airport, then driving the six plus hour ride to Mimi's house. The holidays have not always been something that meant something to me. They have not always been enjoyable or meaningful to me because of my childhood.

The last Christmas I remember having as a family was maybe eight or nine years old. Even then, it was something rushed because of my father either having to go back to work or not being able to come in at all. The last one I remember, was when he drove in with his black Toyota truck, full of presents. It was an absolute scene at the house that day. We only asked for a few things every year. My father would try and make up for his absence by buying us things he knew we would like but never asked for because we were getting older. We found out years before Santa was not real by catching our parents placing gifts out. Thanksgiving was one of the best times of the year for me because of my dad's mother. I never connected with my dad's side of the family, except for Mimi. I related more to my mom's side more. It is where I got my habits that would eventually become my downfall. Holidays mean more to me now. You learn to appreciate everything more, because time demands you to take notice. I hope you have enjoyed my rambling. Love you all. Carpe Diem.

POETRY

Coal

i have been thinking a lot about the title of this book and what it means. letting go of the past and any attachment that could ever be tied to it. the impermanence of life and love itself. the imperfections we all carry around within us. the weight of the world we have given a name to. a promise is never worth holding onto these days. no one can give you what you do not currently have. to find someone simply to make you feel whole will be the downfall for you both. when you are ready to conquer yourself, do not ask someone else how they did it. your survival is not like theirs, but there is hope for us all once someone you come across tells you that they made it out alive. survival guides differ for each individual. make sure you are creating your own and not copying word for word to get you out of a darkness you find yourself in.

Inner Demons

in another lifetime, we chose to stay, and it all worked out. i honestly have seen it and felt it before. maybe this was nothing more than preparation to ready myself. for the times when we cannot accept all of our scars, all of our truths, and all of the love, maybe it was just us passing the time until the end became a beginning we were destined for. i am still learning how to verbalize goodbye, and not look over my shoulder to see if you are looking back at me, too. to see if you hesitate before turning away for good.

When We Think Goodbye Is Best

i do not have anymore room on my body for lovers. all of them have left their marks. i am walking in a misty haze, confused and soberly breathing in days when night speaks of her intentions. i wake up covered in her light. it is the only time i forget i am this way. it will not be the last time i try and tell you, i love you.

Take A Ride

your eyes still hold the first sunset we ever shared together. it is there in a hushed moment, all things come surging back to me with you being the first image i see. i will never wish for a million more of anything, but i will anticipate one more time to witness the colors named after you and that iridescent smile you shine with. the one that never knew how to finish dancing to anything that could move you. now, the sky holds more questions than any answers i feel comfortable telling and holding onto. even if you are still around in your own way, it is a little further away than i would like for it to be. with how things turned out, i have the same relationship with the moon because of it. i will never regret loving you. i will regret not noticing the love you had for me leave when it did and not acting on it.

Season Of Vulnerability

this new energy you have is the kind of vulnerability not all of us will ever find. i hope you use it well. i hope you know how beautiful it looks on you when you wear it as you do, with your red, white, or all black outfits. it matches every single motion you become a part of. i could write to the moon and tell her about you, but she has known about you your entire life. step into it all, with a might and an intensity needed for you to know yourself better than you think you already do. i will do what i can from here to make sure you never forget how finding you and your words saved my own breath and outlook on what it is to be alive. you could be nameless, and i would never forget who you are. i could never forget a full smile staring and strangling devils and demons who believe they have the power and prowess to overtake you. you have been steadily working, with a vibrant fluidity behind the scenes, behind every closed door and window to achieve a better sense of the direction you need to go. you are the third eye of every season, of every religion, of every whispered sigh of atonement worth seeking and embracing. you are love's poetry and signature.

<u>*A Painting Worth A Thousand Words*</u>

the last thing you want is for someone to love you. i know, i am just some human who does not know what to do with his feathered hands when they are not typing. when they are not neatly folded or holding onto something that reminds them of you. you are well beyond where i can reach you now. i do not blame you for keeping your distance from anything that reminds you of what you had, of who you were when innocence was something more than the color palette of which you once used to describe your emotions. you do not need anyone right now. you do not need anyone telling you how it will get better, because you know fish-tales belong to the sea where the sea can lovingly dream about a lonely dream on its own. you are the woman of your own dreams. the one you needed when everyone had forgotten about you and what you were trying to say out loud while you were hurting and afraid. i wish i could understand you better, in a healthier way than keeping my eyes closed, awaiting a touch from you that will never come. you belong to the art you make. to the images and words locked away from anyone attempting to know you in a more affectionate way. i could tell you that you were the flowers, but you would grin back at me, telling me how you have always been the rain.

Tiny Cardboard Mansions

there will be days when nothing can hold back what is inside this flesh. but on the day i feel a little more human, i will give a new name to the empty parts of the sky. a new name to a nameless love. a new name for the blind-spots in my life. a stout drink of falsehood adopted by a single parent finally able to accept a new love into their home. after that day, my bones will grow into whatever is left of me. i wish life felt like a cardboard box, full of tiny mansions to give away to those looking for the riches they will sadly never find. in this disorderly world, to locate one's self, you must first lose every piece of love you have ever touched. it is the only way to know without any trace of doubt, what and how it should feel like pressed against your skin without making you bleed for the rest of it.

HOWLING

there will be countless days that test you even after the confession of a softly placed moon in the darkest of skies. the eyes of beauty do not always see what is inside that makes it shine, even after the rain calls on the stars to wash it all away. i know this phase may feel helpless to you. i know the emptiness precedes the truth of how it became real in the first place. an angel's face will not always represent happiness and light. sometimes, it reflects a pain not many will ever know. blue wings carry more than a northern breeze. they are an institution of awareness for what is beneath them. may you know joy again. may you know what it feels like to lay down and not feel a world's worth of weight crushing your humanness. keep your energy cleansed by a refined love only you can give. giving a breath meaning is what love is about. be it for yourself or someone close to you. may your garden lungs one day open again to a newness, to a transformation of soul and ivory. grow with the life around you, just as the howl is born inside of the wolf, penetrating its own cries for mercy against the white light. your bravery is a powerful accumulation of resilience and rebound from your days when your demons did their best to keep your head down. may you never break for anyone who has not been broken before. only they know how it feels to wholly love a lonely existence and come out of it smelling of victory. a closeness is arriving. a jubilant calling will be with you soon.

When No One Else Is Around

there is no fight between evil and good when you have the devil by the throat. it is in that moment you learn how to kill something for the first time. a mind is a dangerous place to leave behind the best parts of yourself. i have not always made the right choices nor given myself proper love and care. i am the last one to receive any form of comfort when it comes to helping someone else. my honesty is currency these days. sometimes, it takes me a while to arrive at a particular place, an abrupt resolution that either hurts me or the one i am with. if i am being truthful, it is not my fault all of the time. we hope things turn out in our favor, with weighted eyes and damaged dreams of what we believe it all could be, of what we all hope it can be. what is meant for you will find you in this life. anything forced cannot be together longer than the pressure applied to make it last. i have gravely broken my own heart more than any kind of love ever could. there is this single and blissful moment of clarity, something made by grinding my paper bones together. sometimes in life, you will find yourself staying at a hole-in-the-wall motel, in some hole-in-the-wall town, writing about some heartbreak you found along this stretch of highway. maybe love and loss are lovers. maybe i am writing about something that does not exist. maybe some of us are meant to ride solo instead of shotgun. i am too old to care about what will happen tomorrow. i just want to write on the loose about something with enough blood and violence that one day, someone will believe me when i tell them i gave all i had for love's slightest of glances. give me coffee, paper, and a typewriter. i will point out the honest ones who ride willingly on the yawning road as if it were a naked canvas where abandonment is only selfish to those who do not fully understand themselves or the reason why they are still here. i probably ate too many suns and moons as a child, thinking i would be full from their energy and parental guidance. my graveyard has too many stones with no names. i stopped etching onto them when i surpassed the age of thirty-one. they are daily reminders to myself of how short this whole goddamn thing really is and how far we have to go in order to outlast everything else. i am not made for everyone. i am barely made for myself, my own human experience down here. i walk a fine line every single day, with a bonfire steadily catching up behind me. normalcy has never been close enough to me to know me. i have dove head first into everything i have ever wanted to begin. my mind has been broken since the day my parents divorced and chose themselves over my brothers and i. whatever you do to me will never be as hurtful or painful as what i have done to myself over the years. you can try your best to torture me with your kind eyes and openness, but i know the difference between what you say and what you do when i am not looking. i will not suffer in order to save face.

HUMAN

i am not ordinary nor extraordinary. i am merely a wanderer with a name, with a face full of light marks all around it where i have sat and stared into things that did not belong to me. things that will never know where i came from or why i love with this fury given to me by parents who never knew how to show it the way i needed it. to me, that is life. it is reality. it is the deepest insanity one can attain. to be loved and have love almost never marry each other is a divorce of soul from body. never give your best to something who cannot sit with you at your worst and see someone being worthy of their greatest efforts given to rid you from such a place. though i may be nothing extraordinary, my journey is the greatest expo for it.

<u>When The Moon Has Your Back</u>

i do not know if i am getting any closer to who i need to become, but being with the moon, she teaches you how stillness allows you to pull yourself up again, a breath at a time. she is the teacher of light and darkness, of how you can be both, and still thrive living in a human world. we are the shapeshifters, winnowing through a forgotten place of love and loss controlling who we are and who we had to be. if we are to get anything right while living here, may it be to love the moon as she loves her phases.

Christmas Morning

if i could lay next to you, as close as the golden sunflower tattoo resting on your arm, maybe then peace would not feel so alone and distant. maybe then, it would not feel like a relentless outsider, instead of being some barren and unknown relative you barely see once a year when Christmas creaks in the attic above. maybe then, sleeping would not need a countdown to bring you back beside me and your hand in my palm. wherever life takes place, i want it to be where you laugh and smile during some random conversation we have in-between an uneventful morning before anything else finds us. if i could hold you for however long it takes to call a life purposeful, that is what i am after. anything less and we are cheating the light that found us.

UNSTOPPABLE

back when it was kiss and tell, truth or dare. when we were too young to give a damn or ever care. no matter what happens in the days that are our lives, we will live free and rope the moon and every star in the sky. they call us the young and rebellious kind. never allow the thoughts of today corrupt the potential of tomorrow. the right way is only the wrong one for those who do not value deconstructing a life to attain a new one that is entirely your own.

Misplaced Memories

i could have loved you more than you had ever
known of love to be, but it would not matter,
because in order to do so, you would have to
let go of what you are currently holding onto.
i can only wish those were my quiet hands
keeping yours close and pressed firmly against
this soul that knows yours so well and its bones
more than anyone who has known the secrets
you told me all those years ago now. they are
still safe, and they will have their own grave
when the time comes for them to go with me.
it is something i have thought about and needed
to do if something were to ever look for me,
they would never find who we were, who you
were for me, when all i had were these words
to make you feel loved, seen, and appreciated.
i do not miss anything about you other than the
times you thought you loved me.

First Player Mode

i could tell you i love you, but i know you

cannot say it back, and if you did, you would

be lying. i am too old for love to still be a game

played by humans who should know what they

want. not what they can get away with.

PROJECTORS

and maybe that is how it ends for some of us,
with our hearts broken wide open and each
other being the reason for the mess it made.
i do not know where the pain goes when it
leaves, but i do know how it feels to get your
heart back right after the beating it took and
it no longer fits where it once did. love creates
angels just as much as it does monsters. i do
not wish to be either one of those in whichever
lifetime this is, even though i can tell you i
already have a few times. i want to know why
humans continually fuck over one another just
because they believe it is all they can do when
they were raised to never see the difference
between holding onto someone's body and
squeezing someone's throat.

Comforting What Remains

come for me. comfort me. find me. love me at
the edges, the wrinkles this life made for me.
i will do all i can to make sure you never feel
worthless, forgotten, or misplaced. when these
arms get around you and wrap you fully, that
will be where we both can let go and breathe
unrefined. it will be our first home together.

Residual Recognition

i think back to our love. before it was ours.
before we knew what to call it. before we
started learning the little details of each
other. i still think about it and wonder if
anyone will ever be able to close their eyes
and feel you the same way i did, and still do.

<u>When It Matters The Most</u>

i still believe in the power of a
handwritten letter. i still believe in
telling someone how you feel the exact
moment you feel it. do not ever waste
an opportunity, a chance, a single moment
you will never get back. goddammit,
please do not cower in the fear that
only exists between your ears.

A Loss You May Never Recover From

i am constantly trying to remind myself that you are not the one i get to tell all of my things to anymore. it fucking hurts not being able to tell you anything as we once did. even if it was a thought of holding your face gently and taking every bite i could out of your neck and shoulders to show you how often and how much these cravings never vanish. but you are not that someone for me these days. i write what i can no longer say out loud to you. in these books, you may still find yourself, but there are graveyards on every page.

Empty Vases

love will never be the death of me. it will be the reason why i keep giving myself to a cause, to the art, to my dreams so they can live on in something more beautiful than the rose i keep in my heart. something beyond the vase i have become for dead parts no longer belonging to their homes. something that holds both water and air to keep what is left of me alive long enough until the sun takes over for the moon.

COCOON

a human's time and love is no place for cowards. do not fuck someone over because you are afraid of it happening to you. life does it already to those who fight like the survivors it made them out to be. let love be what it needs. leave or stay. it is that simple. mind-games fuck up not only their lives, but the ones who come into contact with them later on. you are sabotaging a generation of love, an entire life's worth of work someone has spent doing to believe they are good enough after being told every day, "i wish you were never born."

Silent Nights

you have been quiet lately. more so than usual. i know how it feels to have a million emotions inside of you with them having nowhere to go. you think by talking with someone it can help. you think by sharing some of it, it will allow you to feel better about it all. but some days, doing nothing is the best we can do. the bravery it takes to go on about your day despite your world crumbling and set on fire is a curse only the courageous can raise and lift their hands to. you have been running ever since you were a little one, with a large part of innocence tied into your childlike and rosy eyes, pretending the backyard went on for miles. ever since you began hiding from your parents, you thought it meant you were hiding from all of your problems. you once thought being alone was love, because the ones who knew you would check on you when they stopped hearing your sounds. then when you grew up, you quickly learned it was something entirely different when everyone stopped showing up. i know you wish you could go back and change a few things, but i am proud of you for still finding love in the pain. for finding your own way through what you keep hidden away, and what you feel as though you have the strength to say out loud to those you love.

LUNAR

i am nothing more than a face and name, but i howl at the light as if we were beasts in love. when it comes to being who you are, do not hold back when someone is giving you their all. they have waited many of moons for something as human as you to show their scars and wounds to. when you find someone who has an instinct to stay instead of running away upon showing them your true side, make sure you never forget the day when you learned it is okay to be damaged by life, and still be loved for how it tried to rid you from this place.

First Home Feelings

i do not know if we are destined to get married. some people do not need it. some people are just thankful to have someone who gets them and wants to spend their last day making sure their light stays lit and their memory is one to never dim or fade from life. they can do absolutely nothing, and still have more than most. a kiss goes a long way when you never want to leave their lips. next thing you know, fifty years will have passed, and you find yourself never getting enough of each other. public displays of immense affection is defined as being secure enough in the real world and not caring when others notice. it is why those who do care, end up never having what you two have together. just like a thumbprint, each love is different. wherever her love is, mine will be craving it. wherever she is, that is where my life is.

Beyond The Orange

you are the last bit of sunlight i reach for before the night speaks your name. i stretch my soul as far as it can go, until you pull all of me back in. until you tell me you are not leaving. until you are the home i had went without and could only give me walls and a smile. you are a precious being. one who does not get enough credit for housing the lonely and misunderstood. but i will tell you this now, i have never felt more like a recovered and unbroken man than i do when you are consoling my anxiety and depression, loving them as if they were our children we were never expecting to have. you told me, what is yours, is mine. but you will not carry what i have had to live with on your own. you will not have them break you before we break them together.

No White Flags

i still fight for love, for life, for beautiful moments that had never been my own to claim rightfully. i am after ripened sunsets and sleepless nights with someone i never wish to leave. i will continue being this way. i do not care if you like it or not. my flesh is mine. my bones are mine. my life is mine. you can keep pursuing as little as possible, until your thimble heart becomes full, but i will not go down a coward's death. i will not be devoured by crows and ravens. they know me too well.

GRACE

like snow turning into water and dancing down
the faces of the forgotten, i, too, will find my
way down to a more precious place and not
get caught on feelings or emotions that
have no power over me or might hold
me permanently to their beliefs.

ARTEMIS

you may think you are at the bottom of
every mountain you have faced or tried
to climb, but you are not. you are a gentle
giant amongst mortals. not everyone needs
to be heard to be seen. you do not have to
bleed to know you are real and alive. you do
not need to be any more or any less than
who and what you are now, my friend.
you made it this far, so i know you have
more soul than the rest who gave up and
allowed gravity to do the rest.

Walking In The Light

i do not know if i will ever be accepting of
who i am not, but one day, i will find myself.
i am just thankful to those who allow space
in their lives for who they see in me when i
cannot see anything behind or in front of me.
maybe that is all one needs in order to know
who they are has and will always be enough for
the path they are on.

Jolly Roger

i am more than the blood spilled to get here. i am a castaway from a time ago when humans actually said what they meant. when things were not so goddamn difficult to make work. back then, i was a more than a wanderer. i was a castle made out of the scripture my mother read, though the bible is one of the books i will never own. i was happy she kept herself in the words she read. i was a ship made out of the gifts my father would buy us to make up for the time he was not there with us. i was a broken speck of light, still imagining marriage and kids. i have lost those things, dropped the dead weight, and now i firmly stand on my own two feet, declaring my love for energy and life. i will breathe in and out as the wanderer i continue to be on a daily basis with a face damn near burned off from looking into the sun more than i should have. moderation has always been my Achilles heel with anything that either made me feel better or feel numb.

UNCOVERED

there is no one else i would rather spend my days with than you. with you, years are nothing more than moments when loving was not always easy, but we found a way to laugh about it all and make room for the days when things actually went as planned. all i need in these momentary pauses of eye contact and gentle embraces, is you, and spotless shine.

Properly Placed

i am arranged in a way to constantly feel.
i am not scared of it anymore. i do not need
the alcohol or drugs to minimize or shield
who i am from it. i am accepting of the pull,
of the magnet i am for the strange things
others find no value in.

Victory For Self

maybe i am not as weird as it seems. maybe my body is floating with the rest of the universe. maybe i am not the same as you, you, or you, but it feels good knowing who you are is only meant to be understood by yourself. even if it is a fucking mess, it is still a matter of life. it is still a walking excuse to live comfortably in everything you do, because no one else will ever be able to produce such profound ambitions, melodies, and dreams. be happy with what you discover. a lot of us go years without truly seizing our goals.

Diverged Paths

i still do not know a goddamn thing, but i am feverishly taking notes and jotting down pauses when things conform into a new idea, a new way of life, a new birthing technique for feelings. deep breaths and holding my eyes closed keeps my head above the fragility of my situation. if you were to turn to me and ask me for my notes, i would have to tell you, no. what i am doing will not make sense to you. what i am doing barely makes sense to me, but that is the point. that is the rub. that is not me being an asshole. i am just trying to help you understand yourself and not what i hear, see, smell, and taste. do not copy my human side. it is not for you. you, are for you.

A Sacred Secret

that is when she is at her best. that is
when victory becomes a living thing.
she choked the devil out and made
it back alive with a million beautiful
stories to tell. she needs nothing else
but a playlist and an ocean's breeze to
give her that smile and joy of being
free. wings and all, nothing else can
bring her down.

IRIS

a smile like hers can cure the broken and heal the wounded living under all of the stars in the sky. the keeper of it all. a bravery walks inside of her, a giant she becomes. beyond the gates, she is just as mighty as the sword and gods that hold it. do not use the same marker to color in the rest of your life, sweet one.

THEIA

i hope you always see yourself as
someone worthy of not only having
what you have been without, but remaining
full on anything you have fought to hold
onto. you are the pause right before dawn.
the truest symbol of light and persistence
shaped as the evergreen you are.

AMPHITRITE

she has drowned a few times for the wrong things, but now she knows how to swim with the waves that made her. dry your eyes, pretty love. there are more wars to be won. dry your eyes, angel love. there are more devils knocking down your door. you are not just one, but all of the moons coming back home.

if you are to be with me, my scars and
trauma come with me. if you are brave
for me, i will be brave for you. i am
nothing if not everything i have
survived. rolling over and seeing
your eyes is the only heaven that
exists for the dead i carry.

<u>1999-2022</u>

-Never Before Seen Writings-

3-5-99
Texas

Drunkard

i never thought i could hate someone so much, until i met myself at the bottom of a whiskey glass. truth is, sometimes i drink to hide inside the bottle itself. at least down there, i don't feel so alone. what is meant to be, will always find its way in the end. people can have all the money in the world, and without faith, it is not worth the price tag. don't let the fall break you. love your broken body and put it back together. there is not time to give up. i wish that a world existed where the music i listened to could actually portray a life i am living through these headphones. please, do not judge me for who i am, but encourage me for who i want to be. these words i type are as real as the lives i have had to help carry to their final resting place.

3-23-99
Texas

Sol & Luna

the love that is kept sheltered in-between the lines, allows the paper to appropriately heal. you see, the paper is me. i contain every word that was real. it is a constant battle to keep the feelings on an 8x12 sheet. when all they want to do is jump off the paper and scream your name. back when you were sixteen, you told me that you had been waiting your whole life for me. at the time, i thought it was a bizarre thing to say to someone when we were both so young. as i have thought about those words, i knew your soul was older than mine. for your soul had lived a life before you and i.

4-15-00
Texas

Pearls For Life

love knows when it is ready, and loving you has been an honor. tomorrow we will celebrate 55 years of marriage and bliss, raising two dogs and four kids. love knew what it was doing when it found us. we found it with our first kiss. rest assured my dear, when tomorrow comes we will celebrate 60 years of magic. i have loved you every day like it was the first time you made my heart jump in such a way my soul knew you were the one who would keep it safe. cheers to you, my love, my life, and my ever so beautiful wife. today i saw an 82 year old man open the car door for his 81 year old wife. they are my neighbors, and he does this every time. their love is the definition of forever. pay attention lads. the elderly generation is giving us pearls. she shouldn't have to wait on you. you wait on her at all costs.

6-24-01
Texas

When It Finds You

love is a lot of things and it can be complicated or
it can be just right. all i know is, when it is real, it will
be the greatest thing to happen to you. life is such a
crazy place filled with such beautiful things, including
love. i know some do not agree with such a statement,
but i sincerely hope it finds you. when it does, i hope
you never let go. i also know that love is not always
everything that is good, but it takes going through all of
the bullshit to realize it is not only a precious gift that
should be cherished every day, it is also one of the
rarest fucking things in this world. though at times i
know it will leave you standing naked in the flames,
it can also help clothe you with the words and feelings
we all desire in the end. for me, love has bruised my
heart and almost took every goddamn thing i ever had.
i am not blaming it on the word itself. that would be
the easy thing to do. i took what happened to me and
learned how to love louder, and my heart got stronger
because of it. it is a choice. i choose love over the
numbness this world wants you to feel. even if it breaks
me again, i will never give up on it. there was a time
when it saved me. i will never forget that.

5-8-09
Texas

Halo Of An Angel

flying high upon this place with angel's wings as her grace. there are times when it's hard to find a soft place to land. when the time comes to come down from up above, she will be running because flying wasn't enough. open to the skies, she has fire in her eyes. closed to the world, she has it all figured out. she is a special kind. one that is hard to find. closing her wings, she takes a chance. closing her eyes, prepared for the free-fall in flight. but she's falling. falling back to life and hits the ground running, running in a widening full stride. whether she is flying, falling, or running, she wears the halo of an angel.

5-8-09
N.C./Texas

BUTTERFLY

butterfly, i will miss you when the rain falls. butterfly, i will see you when the rain dries over the sky. i want to know what makes you fly away and come back home. butterfly, i see you in the day light. butterfly, i hope you fly away with me tonight. i want to fly away with you and come back home. butterfly, i do not know why the rain falls. butterfly, i do not know why the day turns into night. butterfly, do not fly away from me tonight without saying goodbye. so here is to the rainy days, and rainy nights, without saying goodbye.

_5-8-09_
Texas

Dear, Sender

i will fly home when deployment is over and know that i will be home. can you wait this long to read a letter that says i will be home. By the time you read this, i will be back home with you. just know when i am off to war, i will be back again. just know if my brothers carry me home, i loved you all along. i loved you all along. just know if i should fall alone, you were with me all along. you were with me along. i will fly home on my feet or on my back. i know i will be home soon. do you have the strength to read this letter that says, "i will be gone. i will be gone?" by the time you get this letter, it will already be over.

6-11-09

Texas

Eyes Closed

i am going to sit right here and write you a letter. i am going to talk to you when i get through with forever. i am going to address it to you somewhere in the future, to remind you of the past we used to have. for if i never see you again, i will always have a piece of paper and pen. it might not be an everyday thing, but it is you whom i will think about when it is love i am in. if you are reading this, it is already too late, for i am already gone because you could not wait for me. i am sorry. if you are having a hard time, just know it is alright, darling. you do not have to cry, because when you go to sleep tonight, i will be writing you in time, going back to where we used to be. it is fast forwarding our lives that we were almost close enough to see. now, close your eyes, and rest your head. everything is okay just as i said it would be. wipe away those tears from your face. this letter will find you in time. i hope you have found your heart, because this letter was written from me, to you, lost in the dark. wherever your journey may take you, just know how much i wanted to thank you. you revived my heart's passion for love and life. even though we did not work out, i know for the rest of my days i am better because of you. slipping from the grasp this society has on me, i think it is best for both of us to go our separate ways. day after day is a constant battle, a frightful mental rage. trying to allow time to remove all of the negativity surrounding me while i speak to the cosmos. cleanse me from the sins i am covered in, and bring to life a soul that was always destined to be entirely whole, instead of fractionally living where the pieces never fit. you looked right through me that night, but your eyes could not see beyond my heart. my soul knew you missed me, because i could still see my name inscribed on yours. she rolled through my soul like the ominous clouds and thunder from my saddened eyes and scattered heart. it reminded me of the nights i would lie awake for hours in my bed, listening to the sounds in the hallways. echoing screams and shadows dancing all around me. she came home with this look on her face, this glow of pride i had never seen before. she said, "are you ready?" i had no idea what it could have been. we never kept secrets from each other. "to be a father!" my heart literally jumped out of my chest and tried to show her the amount of happiness i was feeling. with tears my eyes have never cried before, they rolled down my face, filling every pore with a degree of joy this life of mine had never experienced. we cried together and embraced, allowing our smiles to comfort us. my entire life was built on tragedy and heartache. now, i am finally living a beautiful life we had talked about for three years. after so many failed attempts at having a child, we were given the gift of raising a miracle. she asked me, "are you the jealous type of guy?" i laughed and told her," no mam. i am not. i know what i offer and if you cannot except me for who i am, then i know someone else will." the knot of love i placed on your finger that night has begun to become undone from all of the pressure surrounding it. this is it, our final act. our final chance to tie our lives with the hands of love. if you wish to, i will help you. if you are willing to help me with the life that follows us after this. if you choose to let it fall, i promise i will not catch it and make you wear it. i will peacefully leave you be with your dreams of finding another. someone who is better than me. my search will end, because i had a taste of perfection. anything less is something i cannot hold onto with half of me on the floor, waiting for the other part of my heart to fall. the truth is, i fucking miss you. the way i miss you is unlike the sun missing the moon or the ocean missing the rain. in some ways, it is similar, but it is not the same. this my love, is my painful reality. your absence has my mind, body, and soul missing you. it is so real to me, even my dreams awake from their sleep to speak your name. those four words make my bones ache and my heart scream out for you to come back to me. many years have passed since i have kissed you, but my lips will forever hold your taste. you were you, and to me, that was the most divine sight these eyes have ever seen. you defined sexiness and elegance all with the smile you put on. you wore happiness better than anyone i had ever met. it was more radiant than the sun. our souls continue to dance around the fire in which we have made.

4-12-01
Texas

Weary Wanderer

"oh weary and traveling soul, where will you go when the world is not big enough to hold you?" i replied, "i shall travel the universe and skip stars over the northern lights. drink from the milky way with the big dipper and use the moon for light. play with canis major and meet virgo, my sign. help orion fend off taurus the bull and make my way to the heavens to say hello to all my friends guarding the gates. maybe the universe will be able to maintain my venturesome soul. that is where i shall go. reaching out, i grab a hold of nothing. life has threw something at me i could not catch without even knowing. past experiences and places i have been have been ripped up and tossed to the wind. have you ever tried to write something without writing? have you ever tried to say or explain something but your mouth cannot move and no words come out? people say they listen, but when they listen to you, do they have an expression? when life throws you something, are you ready for the object, or do you seem to let your emotions block it? wherever the end is for me and my future patiently awaits, i hope its ready for my life to begin and my sorrows and troubles be laid to rest. i just want one time for life to give me an opportunity to catch what it is throwing at me. i have held my breath before and found out i could not hold it anymore. i could not wait any longer. i have closed my eyes before and at night they see the things that are behind my closed doors. i have walked alone on my feet without ever needing a seat to rest. i have held on tight for as long as i could hang on. now, it seems my hands are starting to cramp because i was holding on for too long. i have opened my ears and listened for as far as i could hear. now, the words are starting to become more like a mumble in this constant struggle to find what is left after you leave everything behind. my body is giving up it seems like at times, but i think it is starting over, getting ready to throw it back at life. we will see how life will catch what i could never throw, and that is my answer to what will happen and where i will some day go. my arms are marked with scars that were once open for the world to see. though they have healed now, the pain is still fresh and the screams are now hidden deep down inside of me. just because someone tells you everything is okay and they are fine, does not give you an excuse to forever walk away without realizing how easy it is to camouflage sadness with a mask of normalcy. to those who are fighting the demons who try to manipulate your soul, know that i am a survivor as well and together, we shall fight this war against our minds. you will never be alone. even if we are all created to die, live for today and help each other see another meaningful sunrise. two souls holding hands together learn how to dance.

3-2-00

Texas

Feelings Only A Few Will Ever Know

tell me again, darling, how your world crumbled to pieces and i will take these hands of mine and build you something worth believing in. life is nothing more than shards of your past, creating and taking the form of who you are today. let me help you build a future. one where sunsets and sunrises are plentiful and the stars want to wish on you. life will always be more than what the eyes can see. learn to look through all of the illusions, and focus on me. i will never leave you. they say your full life flashes before your eyes as death comes to take you. if that's the case, i see mine in front of me. she is standing there, with her hair laying on her barren shoulders, soaking in the precious sun rays. all of my moments that will flash, will consist of the first time i saw you; our first kiss and up until the last time i said, i love you. for if i should go, allow me to let her know how she was, and forever will be what dreams are made of when love finds you unprepared.

<u>*1-13-99*</u>
<u>*Texas*</u>

<u>**The Moments Of My Life**</u>

we kiss before we even make up, before we wake up. it is a good life. there is a difference between wearing class and having class. do not be the one who is classless. some people are just born cold. no matter how warm your heart is, you will never warm their soul. i wonder what is like to have thoughts so deep, they pull you underneath the sheets, making your life become a dream in a state of ever-wandering. the first step is always the hardest one to take. the last one is always the hardest one to see. it is called blind faith for a reason. i am thankful for your awakening.

Veteran's Day

i don't know why we say, "happy veterans day." in my opinion, to many have sacrificed and given their lives before us. it is not "happy" at all for me. i find myself crying almost everyday, night sweats, and sleepless nights. my night is not anything like my brothers who are getting shot at and killed at this very moment. my heart, thoughts, and energy go out to all still fighting and whomever came home trying to figure out this crazy life that seems to have gotten a lot crazier. the universe only knows why. on this day, i look back on what my brothers and i have done. all the loved ones we had to leave behind and how it weighed on our hearts each day. it is my brothers who continue to fight and sacrifice in order for us to have a day to recognize our lives. for all the military still fighting today, i thank you in every single way. those before me, still fighting or who gave the ultimate sacrifice. i thank you. and do not ever forget it. from the bottom of my heart. i served with some of the most brave, courageous, and dedicated men in our military. to my friends, my brothers, and everyone who has served, i thank you and my family thanks you. to my Marine brothers, we will never forget those we have lost. i love you all like my own brothers. live long, live free, and love life.

_7-8-04_
Texas

The Feathers We Carry

never allow someone else to dictate your journey in any capacity. these moments we carry are too short to listen to those who have never heard your story to allow them to give it an ending they are running from. only you know what color glory is. only you have held death's feather in your hands after chasing after something you thought would give you life. the obstacles are where every sliver of magic hides.

_8-3-03_
Texas

Hide And Seek

demons seek me out. for i am made of fire and earth, wind and water. each and every piece they will never have. a human they will never conquer. a heart they will always wish they had. i am too animalistic for such creatures to believe they can take me to the fire, when the fire made me, fed me, and taught me where monsters come from. the only ones afraid of such things, are those who check underneath their beds, instead of the flames from where we are made.

Through Absence, We Find True Love

i did not have a break down at all. it was only my heart fucking breaking out loud by the mere sound of you leaving me. i remember writing for you before you woke up. before you had any remnants from the day on your body. before any light could find and touch you, i wrote for you. a thousand sentences flood over me, and the only one i try to avoid is the life sentence spent away from you. it is difficult keeping at bay how i feel, but i will do my best for you the same way you once did for me. i remember watching your chest rise and fall. it was then i remembered how to breathe with a gentle ease. keep resting as you need, and without worry for me. i will find my way through it all again, just as i did before you found me.

Blood & Bond

people do not know how much suffering it takes to become who we need to be. they may see the smile, but it still hurts, and will always hurt until the lesson is learned. you must prepare yourself for the fight. all it takes is knowing who you are. every day, you will be tested and possibly defeated. but that is life. we must be the shield and sword without questioning our worth. this is our way. this is our path. this is our war.

Gently Raging

i have become so many things i never wanted to become. i know what has happened to me needed to happen to find conviction in a movement i was capable of maintaining. the needle from my compass is now a necklace i wear. i never wanted direction of any kind. i thought being lost was my purpose, my tangible truth. writing has led me to some of the most beautiful and desolate parts of this country. cheap motels with clean beds is something of a paradox, but luckily, i have only stayed in a few where i could not get underneath the sheets. i have slept in Afghanistan moon-dust before, with camel spiders and Taliban out beyond the walls. being comfortable with an uncomfortable place is not a thing i worry about. i have been in the worst conditions a human could ever find themselves in, both mentally and physically. my aspiring appetite for travel allows for simplicity to be a calling i am homely with. wherever i find myself, i know it is a part of the crowning journey i must endure to get to my next level of consciousness. life and love were not made to be easy. the only commonality between both is the death they leave behind. i have found hangovers to be an extension of overdoing a good thing, and here i lay with you, sober and mindful of how long it took me to clean up that part of my life. my mind wanders and scatters at the first touch of light. living in a darkness you have grown to love and cherish because of what it kept you away from, will always be a challenge for any kind of momentum to find you and begin the first roll it takes to move on. i know one day, i will have to make it an orphan in order to become more than my demons. i wanted to give you a love you never had before. the kind you told me you had written about once before in a journal you had kept years prior to us meeting. i tend to write about love   too often, as if i know how to speak it correctly before it approaches who it believes me to be. there is no such thing as winning when it comes to keeping secrets like an ocean keeps her favorite shells safe from being in someone else's hands. a closeness may be the end of me, but we are all made to perish gently. only our bodies say goodbye. it is the eternal hello that keeps my soul from the withering like a flower born in snowstorm.

<u>*1-6-11*</u>
<u>*Texas*</u>

<u>*Remembering Just To Forget*</u>

i will have to remember you for longer than i loved you. the open road never relinquishes its power over who you are searching for. the bottomless nights when stars disagree about space and time become an epiphany of sorts for the blind parts inside of me. i take each day as it comes because i once gave up everything and almost succumbed to the voices i could not distinguish or run away from. this beat inside of my chest once belonged to you. it was a calling you ran to. one i could not stop from happening. we were youthful during a time when everyone else was growing up and becoming old and buried within their fears. my skin still reeks of you and your love. it still stretches out to fit around who you made me out to be. i have washed my body over a million times since we last saw one another. i have learned you cannot cleanse yourself of the ocean once you go below her surface. it remains a part of you. even in the ground, it seeps through the earth and creates a new feeling for another to live with. you were a mystery, a deafening pause before a seated eulogy. i looked to you for love when i could not get full off of my own. you were bloodshot skies before my coffee was finished brewing. i remember looking astonished by the way you rose from your slumber, unprepared for the day, but heavily induced with enough beauty to face anything that came your way. there is a rising tension in-between the missing, in-between the breaks and bruising where you had loved me. we never made love, but love made us long before our lips touched. as soon as my feet hit the floor, i am flying. i do not know how to remove myself from a past that has me in a headlock, twisting and ravaging me into an unwanted submission. i scream out mercy, but all it does is cut off more of my breathing. some humans leave us for something better, someone more suitable for the next chapter of a life we thought we would be a part of. my sunset died the day you left me. my sunrise forgot how to reveal a new day when you took it with you. i do not write to relive or rehash what we once were. i try to uncover a grave where you left me, so i can live again. i try to become someone to believe in, a tumbling truth made from a loss that is bigger than any grudge i could ever hold. you will always be a wandering moon in the sky; unable to stay and unable to leave.

6-20-22
Texas

When No One Else Is Looking

i do not want or need sex all that often. i just want you close to me, like a prayer kept safe in its coffin. i write from a remorseful point of view when it comes to you. a saddened day finds me and my eyes begin to bleed colors from a defeated sky. up too early is where i find myself often. a lion's lingering awaits my heart. i am too brave for my art, yet hide behind a sharpened vulnerability disguised to outlast any smile i could ever use to say i am okay with how everything has turned out. i take my hands and move the stars for you. you have not asked me to do that in years, but it helps my feelings when tears become a language no one else can speak back to me. i remember being happy once. it was probably some childhood memory of christmas morning when presents arrived that my brothers and i did not see from the night before. another time i can recall is meeting you in the hotel lobby. we ran to each other as if we had been missing one another for years. a familiarity washed over us, a synchronization of unexpected responses to how we connected as easily as we did. it was something we knew all too well because of how we had grown to become in the months leading up to the encounter that shaped our lives for the next five years. i have tied your memories around the moon. your gravity keeps them there, along with my love for you. i have been in a desolate phase, where the only thing keeping me from running back to you is the ring i did not give to you. i have been weighed down by my emptiness. some days, it feels as though if i move any limb of mine, i will break the rest of me i had saved for this part of my life. getting back to you is a writing i will keep typing and throwing away. it is something i will save for when i make it as perfect as my hands finding your body the first time we touched. we both know the fire we made does not deserve our ashes. a lovely face you are. a comely voice you have. a stoic human you once had to become. i remember stories you told me from your past. those are the ones i will keep safe and away from anyone looking to name my muse. magic only exists when nothing is expected. when no one else is looking but love.

<u>*12-17-01*</u>
<u>*Texas*</u>

<u>*ACROSS*</u>

it all started being a game, but it turned into who would get more fame. sometimes, i would win and other times i would lose and be put to shame. but who can you blame when it is you causing the hurt. all i can do is try my best to make it across the barrier between good and bad. across the lie of who is mad or who is sad. across a line where there is no evil but only good. should i stay or go across. for everything we do, there is a cause for every pause. in life and dreams, what will happen to those who seem to be lost without words and known costs? should they live or die? can they make it across? across the lie of who is mad or who is sad. across a line where there is no evil but only good. should i stay or go across? if only i knew what to do in case something ever happened to you. if only then, would you turn away and say those words i need you to say or would you walk away? if you could not walk those few steps, i would have to say you lost, and it is time for me to get the hell across.

11-16-22
Texas

Ghost Of Us

we may never know of this love again.
the running, flying, out of body living.
i know there is hesitation within your
movements. i know this is still foreign to
you. i know a part of you finds this hard to
believe. i am doing everything i know how
to do without losing myself along the way.
loving someone should never feel like you
are leaving yourself behind in order for
them to find who they are in return.

4-3-10
Texas

Gold Rush

being in the middle of feeling everything and escaping back into myself. some days have a better balance. some days i can look myself in the mirror and say, thank you. struggling through seasons is okay. struggling is what makes the fight in us mature into an educated display of emotional gratitude. when you were made to feel everything, you cannot choose what not to feel. you must sift through it all to find the gold we are all after.

Four Seasons In One

each day will ask something different from you. each day you will die just to live a little more again. the pain is not permanent, but what it teaches us is. wear it in bravery and valor. nay you never run out of the space you need for your own life. may you never feel as though who you are is not who you should be for this season you are in. take your time with love, for love, and your tie for at you find along the way.

5-5-22
Texas

When Time Meets Itself

we all give our best in hopes of it being enough. some days, it never will be, but it should not make you feel any less human. this world needs your effort. it is where the light comes from when too many of us walk in a darkness that overtakes every part of our existence. we are all searching for more truth, more meaning, more of a reason as to why we are here. the dreams come and fade. the days pass before the eyes of the sun and moon. we are all living a life unknown to many, but when we cross paths at times, we should smile more.

6-5-23
Texas

NEVERLAND

i still believe i will run into you when i am supposed
to, when the sun appears in your window and mine.
in my mind, you make up all of the light, which is both
caught and passing though these spaces where my arms
go to hold onto you, but you are not here. not just
yet. maybe i will see you when we both least expect
to find the other. maybe in this lifetime, being together
is worth more than what we have had to leave behind.
i cannot undo all that life has done and given to you,
but i can make you feel better about yesterday, today,
and tomorrow. it took me less than a single day to
know i will miss and mourn you. to know being
someone to someone else makes everything hurt less.
i once thought i was worthless until i had a few
dollars to my name, but that is not worth anything
without seeing your face. i am honestly trying to find
more words to describe me being drawn to you.
sometimes, they are as simple as a mouth being unable
to move, eyes that never blink or become hesitant when
all i can do is place my hand in yours. i still believe
i will find you before dawn asks me if i am awake
or still dreaming.

_4-2-01_
Texas

Repetition Breeds Excellence

some days, all you will feel is defeated before your eyes find reason to even open. on those days, love yourself for the warrior you are, knowing how many willingly and eventually give up. but not you. shine eventually breaks through. tomorrow has become what you thought it never would. new light softer than yesterday props restfully against you. new steps reach out ahead of those jaded feet to guide you home. today becomes an inviting muse. today ignites a freshly discovered trajectory. favored are those who are lost. blessed are those who wander. i may never know anything more than writing words down to explain how one human has survived for this long. i may never be able to write anything but your name, but i will find love without repeating mistakes.

10-24-13
Texas

The Storms We Are Born With

i know all of this will pass, the undreamed breaking, the self-loathing foaming at the corners of the coffin. love is in the moments when nothing feels right, but everything still stands. do not let the idea of who you hope to be with interfere with who wants to be with you without reasons needed. the only thing worse than regret is the absence of love all together. over the years, i have learned that i cannot keep beautiful things. they always wake up one day and leave me for something better. something that can make sense of their quiet struggles. something that can understand their runaway lifestyle. i have tried to be a stoic shelter for them, but they insist on staying out in the weather that made them because a storm becomes everlasting once you feel the thunder existing within their eyes.

Breaking Barriers

may your heart feel love today. may it be loved today. may the worry and fear living inside of it be cleansed and washed from your name. love and be love. everything else can wait. there may never be more than what we feel today for what we love. i often retreat back into myself when i feel more than i have to give. may we all find love in our bravery to go beyond our own walls.

2-14-22
Texas

A Home For Us All

today, become a love you cannot live without. become a giving force of strength and resilience. become a single sun burning for the moon inside. the truth is, I still feel your touch when the ind breaks against my body. you will remain the moon's soul, glowing, gleaming, and full of nutritious light. days will be bright again, by the light of old endings and beginnings. carry your wings deeply and within the heart of yours, within the song of your bones. rest and relax into the whisper being expressed by the birds. the nest of all living things resides wherever your peace can breathe in dawn's first hello.

Beyond The Light

there is love out there. even if it becomes something i will never have again, there is proof beyond the flesh. all i can do is hope the image of the real me exists within these words for you. i remain holding both of my hands full of hope that it is you beside me when everything else falls from my body and is buried with the same earth we found and made love on. i know who you are, and i can only hope these words give you something you can call your own. love becomes a feeling once your souls asks your heart to come back home. it becomes meaningful once the ache becomes tangible for a human who knows which star you always find first, as you look up to know who they are, and they look down at you to remember what you mean to them.

2-14-22
Texas

GIVER

today is love. tomorrow is love. next week is love. next month is love. next year is love. do love with everything. do everything with love. we are made from it. i have loved, love. even in its absence from me. even in the hidden messages within the numerical signs and stars. it taught me to escape this reality, you must trust something only present in those who are present in their own lives. you must believe a greater purpose awaits you, while you sit in darkness for days at a time with only feelings given from within to give back to the light.

2-10-21
Texas

ADAGIO

be with me, now and eternity. there is no me without your breath. without your sugary hands holding my lungs. you are the song of an early morning robin before the sun becomes a father. carry me with you, a i carry you with me. you will never be without this part of me. fade into me. shine a light for me to see. friends become lovers, this is as true as the year bleeds into parts of my shallows. i will hold onto you until we are scraps resting on aged earth or ashes running with the wind. you have always been the strongest. you are just now seeing why and how it knew this. love is a creation. it is a series of randomness disguised as chance. love is a coming home of lost and forgotten children. where kids become adults and they finally get to meet themselves. this is our best version. this is a new starting point of us. slow and steady we will go. leisurely and level we will love again.

5-14-20
Texas

With All That Is Left To Say

being out here has shown me i still have so much to learn. during my best moments of breathing, i ponder how being with someone in the same place, with specks of sun dotted around us would be what could keep me leveled off and fully engrossed with life itself. with all of that being said, undo me down to the bones. untie me down to the roots of my soul. i will never be who i am unless you take me now. my release becomes more about my love for you than anything else around me. love has felt my pain, but what I have to give will never remain out in the open, as it awaits more rain to wash away what you have already laid to rest.

<u>*8-4-21*</u>
<u>*Colorado*</u>

<u>*Pocket Journal/Page 24*</u>

the ducks rest with a breeze giving their minds
a peaceful withdrawal from worry. the grass is
more vibrant here. the sky is more neon.
everything is brighter when you take a
second to witness real life happening
right before your eyes instead of focusing
on a past unwilling to let you go.

_8-4-21_
Colorado

Pocket Journal/Page30

i wish there was a better way to get you back.
i wish you wanted me as much as i do you.
i wish this was not me writing about you still.
some lovers never leave. they just kill you in
the process. some learn how to corrupt your
heart and mind into believing it is only them
who can keep both calm and full at the same
time without ever giving you more. i wish
this was not me still writing about someone
who would rather see me suffer than tell me
it will be okay, or say anything at all for me
to know it was worth it in the end. but today,
you are the furthest thing from my memory as
i watch nature swallow my soul whole.

8-4-21
Morrison

Pocket Journal-Page 33

dance with the sun. sing your song
and give all you can to the soul inside
of this life. more dreams are on their
way. be present. be alive. fully, full,
and fulfilled. be completely present
wherever you find yourself. take in the
sounds and colors of this day as if they
were made just for you. there is nothing
better than hearing the first sounds of
nature in the morning.

8-4-21
Morrison

Pocket Journal/Page 39

we are the light of all things. we need to enjoy
the days as they find us. enjoy the moments and
trust in all things that are unfamiliar with us.
be open to it all. you never know where your
calling will be. listen to the voice that tells you
to go further. it will never lie to you when it
knows you are in need of something more than
waking up in the same place, unable to find a
way out to the new fields of tomorrow.

<u>*8-2-17*</u>
<u>*Mustang Island*</u>

<u>*Leather Journal/Page 53*</u>

we stood by the waves and wished to be swept
away where a breath can be saved for another
life. you are the forever star in my chest.
burning the night in all phases. conquering
the heavens with a single kiss. beating for the
universe and all of creation. we are the sign
of all things to come

5-30-13
Texas

Moon Journal/Page43

looking up at the stars makes you understand and appreciate what art can truly be and how it can impact your life moving forward. we are a conception of all things living. regardless of how small we are inside of this cosmic shifting, our reach is gargantuan.

5-31-13
Texas

Demo Day

do not ever envy someone else's life. you never know who is doing the same looking at your life. appreciate yours for what it is. not for what it is missing. my life will never be for a kind of love that does not lose their minds when it comes to kissing wherever and holding whenever it is needed. if your love is lacking effort and affection, stay the hell away from me. my age is not how i feel, but it does tell me if you are not bringing fire to the table with me. my appetite does not call for watering. it calls for obliteration in all areas of passion.

2-14-19
Utah

FLICKERING

love is you running into my arms each day the heart speaks about an ever-aching moment of being away from you. you are the light in every room. the embrace and clutch needed when all of this breathing is too much to keep inside. my entire body is disheveled, even the energy around my soul is in shambles. but i hold on, because you say my name, and i am brought back to the moment before breaking.

_12-15-22_
Texas

You Over Everything

may you always believe in magic, in the power
of a sunset right before a single tear falls.
life is too short not to indulge in what we feel,
need, and desire. at the core of who we are,
is a subtle act of love and emotionalism,
all entangled in a display for the world to
see how deeply our soul runs in everything.
may you never forget who you are as the day
erases away years of expectations. they are
simply there for us to be reminded not all
things rest where we want them to. we are
a readjustment to the spontaneity searching
for a reason to never settle for normalcy or
anything under a moribund sun. you are the
northern lights. not just a pair of fluent eyes

When Having Nothing Means Everything

i hope you never forget why you started and why you are still giving your best to the hell that often finds us whenever our worries seem to vanish long enough to forget that we once belonged to them. our wings are only given so much power until our bodies must take over for them. it does not make us enervated. it makes us more surefooted of performing when everyone else's act is up and we are able to see through who they have been their entire life. take your advantages early and often. go well beyond your own fight, your own mind, and your own story. be prepared to lose it all to gain what matters most to you.

_6-9-09_
Wilmington

Personal Journal/Page 78

i turned off my phone last night so i did not have to hear another excuse from her. she is starting to distant herself more since we talked for the first time i got my cell phone, but she always said that it would happen that way. she just does not understand love, relationships, or consideration. that is fine. what does not kill you makes you stronger they say. i think i am getting stronger every day. she brings it on herself and does not know how much of an impact she has on my life. it should not have came down to this. she fucked me over so many times, but love was always there with us. her games and fucked up ways were something i liked to play. my heart is gone for now. she already burned a while through it. i used everything left i had. now i will live life as if i have something left to give, when in actuality, my heart is just now beginning to refuel. friends or not, she is the devil but can play the angel. she cheated on me and broke me, why do i still talk to her?

**-part of a song my friend and i wrote in the
Marines that i partly finished when i got out
and found writing again-**

i remember breakdowns and beach towns, bleach blondes and the music loud. cold beer with great buds and the memories that were made there, with waves in the background and music drowning out loud. girls everywhere. parties all the time with no end in sight. these memories come back to me all the time. late nights and good times, laughter filled the air and made everything seem alright. but these are the sights and sounds of yesterday. i remember slow nights and fast times. leaving behind all that felt right. now they are out of sight. until then, i will remember them. open your eyes. open your ears. for tonight might be the last time. years have all passed us by. all we have are memories of the sights and sounds of yesterday

6-23-02
Texas

CONFUSED

it is one of those words for disarranged people, confused i feel. words cannot make one heal. i am too lost to come back. please forget trying. i am long gone. i am not coming back. try all you want, but all you will feel is the pain i have been ill with. confused is so much pain. it is like the rain falling out of a day when the sun shines with vertical rays of light that misses every part of who you are. make all of this shit go away. the life i have lived until now has nothing but hell. i feel abused mentally, but the only handicap that pursues me is the word, confused. make the confession, and leave me. make the pain escape and attack someone else. i cannot take more mourning. i cannot take these fucking mornings when i have to wake up bewildered and tired of trying, of being shut down by the ones who supposedly love you. i cannot take this shit. make it fucking stop. stop this pain. stop this confusion. make me useful, and not confused.

<u>*5-27-09*</u>
<u>*Wilmington*</u>

<u>*Personal Journal/Page 101*</u>

my first day at Wilmington Treatment Facility. it is
different. a lot of people have serious problems here.
mostly Marines here. i met a guy who is Army Recon .
we became friends right away. it is going to be a test
not just mentally, but emotionally for me being here.
XXXXX, i am sorry for everything. please do not give
up on me. i love you.

Wilmington: Day 3

i do not know what is going to happen to me. i am kind of freaked out of my mind. everyone here has either been really bad off on drugs, or like me, alcohol has damn near ruined their lives. whatever happens to me, i know it is meant to be. life up until now has not been perfect by any means, but it seems to be getting harder. i miss XXXXX so much. i will never be able to tell her enough how sorry i am. i wish her the best always. my life is at a standstill now. i am not sure what will happen or what i will do. please be with me through this trying time. allow me to get back up on my feet and walk out of here a changed man. for all the wrongs i have done, there have been right ones along the way. it seems and feels as if all the bad i have done finally caught up to me and bringing me all the way down to a rock bottom where i sit with, writhing in my pity, sadness, anger, dismay, and broken state.

<u>5-29-09</u>

<u>Wilmington: Day 2</u>

i am missing XXXXX more than ever. i do not know what is going to happen. i have less than a month left here, but it is groundhog day every day at this place. i wake up, drink coffee, and smoke cigarettes, then more cigarettes, eat lunch, talk a little bit to those i am getting to know better, smoke more cigarettes, then read some pages from the bible i was given, then watch whatever television i can. eat dinner, and more cigarettes, then go to bed around 11. we wake up at 0630, and do it all over again. i just want to talk to my dad and XXXXX. i love her so much. i never meant for this to happen. they say that god works in mysterious ways and you will not understand why things are happening the way they are. it feels as if my my faith and self-responsibility are being tested. i am shackled it seems. i have never allowed myself to be helped or for myself to get my problems straightened out. for all i know, this is where my life will either start again or remain at rock bottom with everyone else who thought it was too difficult to ask for help. i think back to when i was in high school looking towards my future. my life was horrible and hellish then, but i never expected nor saw this happening to me. but now, time is all i have, and i am running out of options. it is mind-blowing to think that this is only day 2 of 28. please be with me and protect me from harm. i know my wrongs. i want to make them right.

Day 3

i got up at 0530, drank four cups of coffee, and just thankful for the day. i talked to XXXXX last night for about an hour and a half. we straightened most things out between us. we both understood that we needed each other and that love comes first in our relationship. she cried, and i said what it was i needed to tell her and had been meaning to tell her ever since it all happened. we are not engaged anymore. i think it is better that way for now. our love is stronger now considering we went so long without talking. i love her, whether she is mine or not. we both know we will eventually marry.

Wilmington Day 6

i went to bed around 2140. i was pissed off thinking of XXXXX. something she said pissed me off and i woke up at 2345 to use the bathroom. she called around 0100. i pressed the ignore button because i knew she had probably been drinking. i did not want to talk to her in that state of mind. i woke up at 0545, depressed and not feeling like doing anything, but it is another day, which is a gift for myself. i am doing my best to make the best out of this situation i put myself in, while my friends are all out there enjoying their break. i am trying not to talk to her during the day while i am here in rehab. it makes everything a million times harder for me, but she does help me in the same breath. it is weird that one day is one way, and the next, she is totally the opposite. i comprehend bipolar extremely well. i never realized it until it was too late as to how similar we were and how naive i had been to all of it. sometimes, love makes us the absolute worst version of ourselves for the sake of keeping everyone happy and everything the same. i just want to get back in the real world around my friends.

GIFTS

poetry is made to messy and misunderstood.
for our brains and thoughts are of our own.
to find humans that understand the words in
which you try and convey, is an explosion of
dying stars that is hard to fathom. creating and
birthing an idea not only you believe, but others
do as well. in order to believe in yourself,
you must first believe that your wishes have
never gone unnoticed. i loved you so much that
i wanted to bring you everything everyone had
ever taken away from you.

The Best

when it's all said and done at the end of the day,
it's you i see, your smiling face. it's a reminder
to me that all things can be more than a dream
if you open your eyes to see. it is you who has
been standing there, waiting on something,
more than a chance, similar to a dare. whatever
happens at the end of my day, it all comes full
circle at night when my dreams of you come
into play. they are all in my head. i cannot get
them out, just like you in the morning, trying to
get out of bed. when i fall asleep, i want to feel
your cold toes on my feet. i want you to feel
my body giving off its heat. it is the simple
things in life we all take for granted, when
it is the hardest things to try and plan them.
wherever this life takes me and wherever i go,
just know the sound of your voice is something
i will always know. days come and days
past, missing you it seems is always just that.
my missing thoughts of missing you is

sometimes all i have at night. when i wish they were really you. i can see you all the time and i can hear your voice throughout the minutes that past, but just know i will make them last. i just want you to know if something should ever happen to me, that no matter what we have been through, you were the best thing that ever happened in my life. through it all, great and the worst, the bottom of my heart, i loved you the most. i love you beyond reason because the only thing i needed was you. i hate what i did, but i hate how you made me feel for it. i hated you for the longest because of it, i knew i was the reason behind your frustration and anger, but if you only knew how much i hated myself, you would have known i was halfway between life and death for a while before committing all of my life to work on my own needs and life.

<u>*2-9-06*</u>
<u>*Texas*</u>

This was a concept for a novel I thought of and never had the time to finish it. I believe I got to chapter five before stopping.

For a lot of teenagers, youth is the time for experiment, time to step into their own identity as an individual, not just a student. For most of the young teenage freshman it's a time for panic and uncertainty, not just in freshman English class, but as a 14 or 15 year old boy or girl. So much is riding on these four years of these young students that sometimes pressure is more than they can bear when it is coming from not just inside the school, but in their home life as well. Growing up can be a difficult transition for a young adult, especially when academics might not be your thing, but you're a God at sports. That can also be switched around and broadcasted by the parent who could have been, but now he or she is that overbearing parent who is living through their children to succeed at something they failed to do some years ago. For Tristan Reynolds, high school was merely a stage, a prominent starting position to excel in all three varsity sports that had brought him fame and glory as a young teenager in Waco, Texas. Tristan Reynolds was born and raised in the city of Waco. A very talented and gifted athlete in pee wee football, little dribbler's basketball and baseball, Tristan's parents knew they had something special. Tristan's father, Larry Reynolds, had raised his son to be the best at everything he did while he was younger. To this very day, Tristan's senior year and last year as the starting quarterback for his team, he knows what is coming next, basketball. For it is his all time favorite, even as a young boy. Basketball has always been everything and more. It showed when Tristan started making all-star team after all-star team while involved. By his freshman year in high school, Tristan was already starting on a prominent Varsity squad. After earning All-American honors his sophomore and junior year, Tristan was being contacted by numerous of D-I schools. After finishing his final game in the State

Championship, Tristan turned his focus and main efforts to basketball. His team was ranked number five nationally. They had all of their starters coming back, including the two time All-American. They were on a roll, sweeping every tournament they entered by an average of double digits. Tristan was having the season only dreams could make up. He was averaging over 25 points a game, five rebounds, and eight assists. Scouts were drooling all over him and dying for a chance to get an opportunity to get a moment of his time. Finally, after mid way through the season, with only a few games left, Tristan was voted as one of the finalists for Gatorade's National Player of The Year honors and was invited to play at the McDonalds All-American game. Even with all of the accolades, the young man was putting up the only thing on his mind was winning the state championship and attending college after words. As the season came to end, Tristan and his teammates were raising the state championship above their heads for the final team as players, teammates, and as friends. The season was capped off by an astonishing 29-0 record and 4-A Texas State

Champions. Tristan received the MVP of the tournament while averaging a state record 42 points per game. After the hoopla and media frenzy was over, all that stood between Tristan's dreams were that of his father's, the family business. Larry Reynolds took over Reynolds Reality, while Tristan was still a young boy. It had been in the family for over 30 years. With the decision of his life to make, whether to stay home or venture of into his own dreams and goals he set as a kid, Tristan will wait till the right offer to make his move. The summer of national signing day has given Tristan plenty of time to make his decision. With his family by his side he makes his announcement. "I, Tristan Reynolds, will be accepting an offer from, Syracuse University, and will be attending in the fall to play basketball and football." The whole gym erupts as to what just happened. The crowd is screaming "Thank you, Tristan! We knew you could do it." While the crowd had sensed his decision, his father grew weary and astonishment was all over his face. On the inside he was furious, about to hit the roof, yet on the outside he remained calm, cool, and collected for his son. For the decision his son just made, unknowingly just cost him his father's love and friendship. While growing up in Waco, Tristan and his two brothers Rex Reynolds age 21 and James Reynolds age 15, were all caught in between a custody battle between their parents. Both father and mother knew what this would do to the family and how the kids would eventually treat each one of them, if they decided to go through with it. But it had come a time to cut off the loose ends and move on with their lives. So the battle began and for about 6 months of confronting each other with the idea of custody of all children, they both decided that the only right thing to do was to leave the kids in school where they were at and leave it at that. Tristan was only 13 years old at the time. Not knowing what really happened behind the scenes made himself that he would never do that to his family or ever leave his wife no matter the situation that came about. One rainy Friday evening, Tristan came home late from basketball practice his freshman year. Only to his astonishment to find his mother black eyed and bleeding from her lip. Tristan ran over to his mother and asked "Who did this to you?" His mother, Regina, did not reply. So he asked her again, this time raising his voice a little more assertively, "Who did this to you!" She looked at him with tears and mascara running down her face, and said, "Son, your father did this." Tristan got up and ran to grab a baseball bat he had not used in over ten years. He took it from its spot in the corner by his bed and down stairs he went. When he got downstairs, he saw his other brothers already waiting on him. Their mom had told them that Tristan was going to do something he would regret. So with bat in hand, Tristan asked them, "Where is dad?" Nobody replied. They just pointed into the direction of the shed out back. Tristan went running as fast as he could with bat in hand and knocked down the door with a swing of the bat. Tristan at age 14, was already almost six feet tall and pushing 175lbs. At the end of the shed was his dad, with a handle of Jack Daniels, sipping away. Tristan knew the consequences of his actions if he actually went through with his plan, so instead of hitting his father, he threw the bat in the direction of his father, knocking some random tools off the shelf,. He then looked his father in the eyes, and said, "What you did to mom, what you did to our family, just know that whatever happens to us, to my brothers, know that I hate you." Then as quickly as it started, it abruptly ended that night. Since that incident, the Reynolds family has overcame most of the turmoil caused that evening, but the result was a devastating blow to Tristan and his brothers. After the divorce went to court and was heard in trial, the custody battle was over and each Larry and Regina Reynolds would be allowed to see their sons, but the overall custody was given to their father, Larry. That decision left a bad taste in Tristan's mouth and ever since then he has despised his father even more and tried to excel and succeed in everything just to get away from Waco. Regina eventually moved down to Houston, and married into money by means of the oil field and some old oil tycoon. The communication barrier that was built throughout their 13 years of living together was finally broken after his freshman year at high school. It would be almost four years later when his mom was reading in the Houston Chronicle that her son had verbally committed and signed a letter of intent to play at Syracuse under coach Jim Bohiem. Regina never missed the news, because her son was in it all the time. MVP of the state championship, three times All-American, and voted by the coaches as Gatorade's National Player of the Year. Regina knew of her son very well. Tristan's brothers were never as good as him in the athletic department, but they were both gifted and over-achieved in the academic department of their school. Dating back as far as Tristan could remember, pickup games between his little brother James always prepared him to become what he eventually turned into, a superstar. The basketball court Tristan grew up on was made of grass and dirt. The goal was a shanty of a basketball rim and backboard. It always gave them both the roughest of times, but in the end, it gave them a lifetime of memories. Rex Reynolds grew up loving football. He, just like Tristan, was gifted at that sport. He loved the game, had passion for the sport, and had a heart big enough to hold his teammates in. If it were not for his senior year at Waco High after tearing his ACL, MCL, and PCL, Rex would have played at the University of Texas on a football scholarship. Though he was injured, Rex was still smarter than Tristan could have ever been. Tristan was coming into his final year holding a 3.8GPA, his older brother and younger brother were both already known for their excellence in the classroom. Tristan Reynolds, all Mr. Everything, had the world in his hands. After making his decision to play at Syracuse on a basketball scholarship, everyone was wondering why Syracuse. Tristan addressed the Waco Tribune after everything settled down to distinguish fact from rumors. "First and foremost, Syracuse is a premiere athletic and academic University. Second, Syracuse was the only college that offered me a chance to play both basketball and football. My last reason was solely based on my own decision as to what it would offer me the best opportunity for growth and maturity. I chose Syracuse because Syracuse chose me." Right after that hit the papers, his father got a hold of it. Larry did not always know what his son's intents and purposes were in life, but he knew Tristan loved basketball and football. Larry was starting to get ready for work one day when all of a sudden he felt this sharp, intense pain on his right side of his chest. He winced in pain and it was so severe, Larry could not yell out for help. Larry Reynolds went into a state of panic and horror that morning, without getting the attention of anybody. James had heard his father rummaging around up stairs and heard a thud only something with some weight to it could make. Not in a hurry to get up the stairs, James finally approached the open door and ghastly image that was his father lying there, white as the sheets on their bed. James yelled down to Tristan, "Get up here! Hurry! Dad is having a heart attack!" Without any hesitation, Tristan was already in the room before James finished. Tristan told James "Call 9-1-1!" The ambulance arrived 15 minutes after the phone call. Larry was rushed to the Hospital, having been brought back to life three times while on the ride over, he was in critical and unstable condition. Tristan and James called their older brother Rex who was out of town on business that dad just had a heart attack. Rex said "I am on my way". When Tristan and James got to the hospital, their father was not breathing. With tears falling down their face, both yelling and screaming, "Dad, I love you! Do not go! Dad do not go! We love you and we are sorry!" The tears and screaming antics were more than enough for the hospitals other patients, so they were escorted into another room. Just as one of the guards on duty tried to close the door, Tristan leaped for the door knob, pulled the door open, and crushed the guard behind it. James followed, and yelled, "Get to dad!" When they got to their father, he was not breathing. Tristan thought back to when he threw the bat at his father, when he disowned him that very night. When he would never have the respect or show the love for his father that many fathers deserve. The flashbacks kept coming for both son's, but the flat line was telling the real story. The doctors were still working on him. Rex had finally arrived after being absent for most of the duration. Rex took one look at his father's ghostly white image and tears came running down his face. The man that all three brothers despised and hated for so long, but had raised them to be the best at everything they did, was now lying motionless on the operating table with tubes coming in and out of every hole in his body. Suddenly, the flat line started to spike, the doctors did not get there hopes up. Larry had been dead four times with signs of life every two to three minutes. Their father was the doctor's miracle patient, and he was alive. As soon as the three brothers heard the heartbeat spike again, the tears started and the frowns and gloomy sighs were replaced by a resurgence smile and a feeling of hope. After five minutes of the heartbeat spiking and the blood pressure catching up to the heartbeat, the three brothers knew their father had achieved a miracle and a status of a man unwilling to go and leave behind so much unfinished business. As soon as the news of their father's close call got around to the other family members, their mother was there by the next day. They both left on terms many would never mend, but a close call with death cancels out all of the hardships and misunderstandings over the time that they were divorce. So with their father moved from ICU into a normal boarding room, the family of Tristan, Rex, James and their mother Regina, disgust what each should do. The decision and sacrifice they make will be the deciding factor of Tristan's collegiate career.

1-29-10
Texas

Airport Goodbye

sitting here, watching the people come and go, leaving the ones they love to another trip into the unknown. as i used the phone, it seemed like my heart was about to beat out of my chest. i guess i miss you more, and i still get nervous leaving behind what seems like a million lifetimes. it is going to be unlike any other goodbye. this time, i want you here with me tonight. i am writing this as if i can see you in front of me. i guess i see you everywhere i wish you could be. in the morning, i will be leaving. in the months to come, it is you i will need.

1-29-10
Texas

This Is Not Goodbye

has it come to an end this life that i have lived? for three long years has come millions of tears and millions of fears. i have lived a life many would envy. i have lived, loved, and once had "the one" people speak of. she is out there tonight, maybe wishing on this star. maybe tonight, i can go to sleep tonight. this pain that resides in my chest, this lump that is in my throat, it's going to be hard writing an end to this note. maybe one day, there will be no need for a goodbye. maybe one day, i will have you to say goodnight. until our time, just know this is not goodbye.

1-29-10
Texas

Why Is It?

why is it we love, knowing the chance of it
falling through and breaking your heart into
a million pieces is right around the corner.
why is it that we trust, knowing after every
breath we take there is a chance of loosing a
friend over a misunderstanding. why is it that
we care for those we cherish, knowing there
will come a day when those we love, trust,
and cherish will leave us. why do we love?
because love is the only thing people want.
trust is earned, not given. our loved ones were
created for us. love is the most powerful gift
the cosmos has allowed us to seek and share in
someone. i love you, because there is nothing
more to lose than your mind and heart.

8-19-14
Texas

Limbs Of Life

i have come to the realization that i may never
have the opportunity to love you again, and that
is okay. once was enough for a thousand
lifetimes. i understand a love like that does
not happen to everyone. at least we had it.
when i think about you, i think of all the times
i was lucky enough to call you a part of me.
now, you are nothing more than a limb i never
use, an extremity of death that leaves me
whenever i sit down to write.

MIDNIGHT

there were rose petals leading from the front door to the bedroom. when she got to the bed, there was a note that read, "if you are reading this, please make yourself comfortable." she undressed down to her bra and black lace panties. i slowly opened the door and saw her in the candle light. it was a night when i knew shadows would dance on the walls and ceiling, trying to keep up with the sights and sounds of reality. i touched her shoulder and she smiled, as she looked up at me. those eyes could read the words written on my soul. i leaned in and kissed her. she met me halfway with her merlot laced lips. i began to drink her, sip after sip. as the moonlight peaked through our window, i saw what she had wanted to do ever since she read the note, and that was to be comfortable. i took her hand and placed it over my heart, allowing her to feel the reason why i was here with her while we were alone together in the dark. our eyes locked at midnight and the shadows were gone. all that was left of the night was two humans, walking on the walls, hand in hand together.

Bukowski & Me Part 1

they try and tell me that life goes on. well to them it might, but to me, nothing is quite as it seems. reality is our soul's perspective on life. while on the other hand, i prefer to dream. my unconsciousness is where i would like to be. asleep for the universe so my demons do not bother me.

9-15-12
Texas

Bukowski & Me Part 2

i once knew a man who had all of what life could hand him. his name was Charles, but he preferred me to call him, Charlie. he lived behind the liquor store on broad street, in a dark and infested alley made up of garbage cans and cockroaches. it was pretty fucking miserable to see it with my own eyes. the man only owned two things in life now. one of which, was his white chuck t's and he wouldn't be shy to tell you how damn proud he was to have them. the other was a green and white starter backpack filled with notes and letters from the life he lived before. i never understood why he never had his shoelaces tied though. maybe that was all of the freedom he could afford. later on that week, i decided to get on my bike and pay Charles a visit. i will never forget that Sunday morning. the birds were chirping, because another day had come and the cold front from`the night before gave the leaves this ominous presence about them as they fell over me. i arrived just in time i thought to give him the clothes i had bought him from the allowance my parents gave me for helping out around the house, but all i found was a note.

8-29-14
Texas

Bukowski & Me Part 3

the walls still hold inside of them the screams of my younger days. a childhood of giving thanks to them, because they were the only things that could protect us from her anger and angst. every time i go back to that god forsaken place, i still here my screams and cries of yesterday. i still see every episode that almost kept us from ever growing old with regret for not being able to take up for ourselves.

8-29-14
Texas

Bukowski & Me Part 4

the cold truth is, i am scared to have kids. i am scared because of the life i have lived. maybe one day, i will see beyond all of my failures and mistakes, understanding that a baby is a miracle sent from my past to replace me. i have lived with this fear for a long time and i have been wishing for even longer that maybe, just maybe, the universe will have mercy on my soul when i bring a baby into this world.

Bukowski & Me Part 5

it was a day unlike most. the first thing i did was turn on the tv just for the noise. my mind seemed to work better that way. the more chaos, the better. off to the bathroom i went. first, i had to shower. there is something pure and innocent about water drops cleansing your soul from the night before. i hope heaven has one. after i fogged up the mirrors, i had to use that old brown hand towel on the second shelf. i proceeded to shave when it dawned on me that today was not a work day. i thought for a minute, "Dammit! Let's celebrate this day. if for nothing else, let's drink for another day with our feet hitting the floor!" i put on my favorite Aerosmith t-shirt and sweatpants. nothing says "i don't give a fuck" like sweatpants. i mean, who really wants to go through the hassle of ironing jeans or trying to find a polo with perfect symmetrical seams.

as i walked out the door, i heard an old lady say something from room 202, "i hope you have a wonderful day, Jack." she always remembered my name. though for the life of me, i never cared to remember hers. i know she would like me to reply, but sometimes, life makes you forget the simplest forms of goodbye. i smiled at her and went on my way. my mission for the day was simple. advance to the liquor store, by $50 dollars worth of whiskey, and this time i will be sure to buy something for me to eat. last time this happened, i ended up in my lonely apartment, curled up next to the staircase.

<u>6-21-14</u>
<u>Texas</u>

<u>You Are</u>

you are the reason why my heart still beats. you are everything around me that strengthens me. you are the whisper in my ear when i cannot sleep. you are the brightest star and the only one i see. you are the one who my heart plays for. you opened my eyes by opening my soul. you are the lifeline i needed when i thought of letting go. you are the memory that plays every day. for all of these reasons, i am thankful that we met that life-changing day.

<u>*1-8-15*</u>
<u>*Texas*</u>

<u>*XXX*</u>

as my hands found her throat, they began to glide down her unclothed body. from her neck, they moved to her breasts, and then traveled down to the jeans she was wearing. i slowly used my fingers to unbutton her pants and i leaned in, kissed her rose colored lips. as our eyes met in that moment, i asked her, "are you ready to play now?" as she nodded, i covered her mouth with my hand, pushed her back onto the bed, spreading her legs as wide as i could make them. my fingers began to run and walk all over her nakedness. kisses followed, and then licks to each breast, each hardened nipple. her body was made for me, and i was going to make sure i did my part to make sure she could hardly walk after our sessions.

5-28-14
Texas

Look At Me Now

she told me to go find myself, so i went looking. i checked under empty bottles and broken glass. then i went to look under my bed of demons where i kept my past. i even looked in the mirror, but he, too, was laughing back. so after searching through a lifetime of years, i finally gave in and bought myself some more paper and an expensive pen. i think now after all i have been through, i can finally tell her to kiss my ass. you made me who you could not stand. listen to these words that i now write, from a man who she said could do nothing right.

2-23-12
Texas

The Walk

there is no steel guitar in this song they are singing. just loneliness and broken hearts play to the crowd. manically roaming around life with a purpose in his mind that nobody else could help him find. raising the only material thing he owns, he raises his lighter to everyone else's phone. the flame is the only light he sees, but it is a constant reminder to him what his eyes have seen. though he has a home, he still feels homeless. in his heart, he understands what sacrifice means, and every day he partakes in this insane society. he cannot buy the life he sees, so he dreams of a life that makes sense. fighting is something he was born to do. not against others, but against others fighting with you. he sees peace on the streets of insanity, envisioning a life that can sustain hope and belief. the two things that are not free in this life, and he has earned them through trials and tribulations. while never entertaining

the thought of the strikes and protests that
embark on the life he sees. he still notices the
signs and faces that make the world's shape.
at times it can seem as if the entire world
is rectangular instead of round because of
the sights and sounds embodying humanity.
life to him is a silhouette of the sky, a constant
reminder that the clouds and stars making it up
are ever changing, and eventually die. walking
miles a day with the same smile on his face,
he sees those with disgust and lonely faces on
those who have a seat-belt to buckle instead of
just two shoelaces. it does not bother him and it
never brings him down, because he knows
what it takes to make a worried day stay away.
finally making a stop to rest his worn down
body and shoes, he takes a notepad out when
others would have opened a bottle of booze.
jotting down periodically throughout his day is
a way for him to escape from this lonely place.
the words have never been read by anybody,
even though he has ran into everybody that is a
part of it. there are more than just life lessons
and day to day routines that happen. he takes
time to write down who and what has made his

day so far and who has turned the other way when asking for nothing more than loose change. he writes "life was not made to be figured out in a day. people were not meant to enjoy life, but to love life. life is not what makes you. it is what you make out of life. people value themselves more than they are actually worth." eventually, the old man gets back to his shack he made a home where everyone he loved has left and moved on. he has no electricity or running water, yet he knows it could be worse. instead, he continues writing for the night and finishes the journal with a thank you, and an amen. the old man is deaf, but still hears. the old man has one leg, though he still walks. the old man never had an easy life, yet he knows the word, easy, was never in his vocabulary. he fought for his country a long time ago. he lost his leg and his hearing some time ago during the war. the clothes he wears are the same fatigues he had with him when he came home. life was never made to be easy. do not try and figure it out. just enjoy what you have.

2-23-10
Texas

The Outside Light

there is a light outside tonight that is circling my mind. thoughts spin through the air as the snow hits your hair as it falls everywhere. the light comes around every couple of seconds and it beckons my call to return from it all. as i sit there and stare, it all becomes clear that my thoughts are of you tonight. i wish you were here but as the light intrudes from my crystal clear vision, my decision is to stop and look. i look at it, and it becomes brighter with the snow making me feel lighter. i hear a cry out in the distant and wonder what they were missing. i wonder if this light could not help them find their way around the torture and abyss of the cold. meanwhile, there i am, lost in translation, feeling the deception by the littering snow that is not even falling. it is me that is falling. i am the one who is lost and trying to find my way back to the light. as i try and open my eyes, the faint light hits the sky. all i see is black all around me. no more light. no more sound. it is getting colder with each minute passing. i am frozen solid in my tracks. there is someone's touch creeping up my back. i see nothing. it is hard to see anything when your eyes keep shutting. but as the touch reaches my neck, i find it hard to account for everything i am feeling. all of it is coming from the light. i cannot tell where the light is beaming from. all i can see are these shadows in front of me with my eyes playing tricks on me. where i once was, i am not there anymore. the light disappears, and i am standing here with my eyes open wide, looking to the sky, and asking myself, what just happened? did i just travel through time? did i just fall over and die? the light outside went away like there was nothing out there but my body of lies. i can still see the light from time to time, but it has never been as bright as it was that night when the light from outside was looking back at me.

Warning Signs

i am finally happy. i remember when i used to say that years ago, trying and forcing myself to believe it. people will pop back into your life in order to try and ruin it. do not allow them to. do not give them the satisfaction. my life is with the one i love now, and that is the only thing that matters to me. if you are not a part of my life and choose to walk away, stay the fuck out. do not come back. my life is better now since i know who truly cares for me. do not play fucking games with me. do not think you can do whatever the hell you want, when you want. this is me telling everyone who has left, stay gone. do not ever come back into or around my life. you have been warned and this is last time i am writing this.

_5-29-14_
Texas

Connecting Souls

to all the lost and broken souls who scour the world looking for love, i say to you, one day, we will live amongst those who find the love these humans speak of. we will relish in its overpowering feeling. until then, we will continue to assist those who need us for help along their way.

9-18-14
Texas

What It Means To Know You

i know everything there is to know about you, and we are still distant strangers. the way you would say, "i love you, too babe." how you would say, "i will see you soon, instead of goodbye." how you absolutely hated the color purple made me laugh. the way you would sing your lungs out in your car and dance as if you were putting on a show for the entire universe made me feel special to be riding in the same vehicle as you. the way you took my hand when i would drive, made my soul jump out of my skin and love you on the spot. how you gave me butterfly kisses truly made me believe we could fly away together. your tickle spots were my favorite. we both knew you enjoyed it though, because it made us love even harder when we were ready for each other. i know it all, and we are still strangers. life is when you meet someone on a random Saturday night. now, i write to make up for the memories we no longer share. i am cursed with our memories making up for a lost life.

<u>11-2-14</u>
<u>Texas</u>

Brotherly Love

this is not a poem. i got kicked out of my home
along with my younger brother when i was a
sophomore in high school. my older brother
was kicked out his senior year by our mom.
our childhood was anything but normal.
though today, i stand taller than most
skyscrapers in the cities, because of the
love and admiration i have for my brothers.

What Life Means When It Leaves

i know i need to let you go. i know you already did several years ago, but you are the ghost story i cannot stop telling others about. i know you moved on while i kept digging you back up to hold one more time, to feel your bones against mine. i have apologized to myself a million times already today for mourning what has been gone and buried. i tend to hold onto things until they become an extra limb to use in my daily living. it has almost been a show and tell of sorts when it comes to you. i know many who have lost something they loved and kept talking about it, thinking it would magically come back to life in front of them. i loved you so much for so long. the absence is only comparable to a sky without light, a human without a heart to give to someone else. you have not kept me from attempting love again. i get both of my feet out of the door, and i am running wide open, floored with something immeasurable to give to someone who has been without what i have inside. i do not know how not to carry around the dead. i do not know how to close books that have left me feeling half-read and abandoned by the seventh chapter. you have been with your muse for almost three years now while i have been writing about one that does not even know what i did today. i need to remain strong enough to outlast everything i am still dying to tell you. your hands do not fit into mine anymore. your eyes do not look at me when you look for your better half. your body does not warm the cold spots in my bed. i was never one for attachments, because i knew they were something that would keep you from your new life should they fall like leaves from the dead trees inside of you. my lungs still carry your name, but the voice i once used to say it died the day your exit almost killed me. i bought a pack of marlboro lights after you told me about him. i kept them packaged and unused for almost six months. i ended up smoking four of them over the course of three months, because i was defeated and fell victim to my own breakdown. i threw away the rest of the pack before i left Utah. it has been the only time i ever felt hopeless because of what someone did to me. goodbye does not always find us, but this is my attempt to give peace to the death of us. it has been my weakest part about me and this new life i am trying to get to. there is and will remain hate inside of me for what you did and how you went about doing it. i remember watching my parents for years argue and fight and hurt each other on a daily basis with their actions. i told myself then i would never be that way. i told myself i would never allow someone to do that to me. i let myself down because i allowed myself to believe you were different, but you showed me how humans will say anything to get their way in the end, with or without having to say a word to do so.